Club Drugs

Karen F. Balkin, *Book Editor*

Bruce Glassman, *Vice President*
Bonnie Szumski, *Publisher*
Helen Cothran, *Managing Editor*

GREENHAVEN PRESS
An imprint of Thomson Gale, a part of The Thomson Corporation

Detroit • New York • San Francisco • San Diego • New Haven, Conn.
Waterville, Maine • London • Munich

For more information, contact
Greenhaven Press
27500 Drake Rd.
Farmington Hills, MI 48331-3535
Or you can visit our Internet site at http://www.gale.com

LIBRARY OF CONGRESS CATALOGING-IN-PUBLICATION DATA

Club drugs / Karen F. Balkin, book editor.
  p. cm. — (At issue)
Includes bibliographical references and index.
ISBN 0-7377-1607-X (lib. : alk. paper) — ISBN 0-7377-1608-8 (pbk. : alk. paper)
  1. Ecstasy (drug). 2. Designer drugs. 3. Designer drugs—Law and legislation.
4. Drug abuse. I. Balkin, Karen F., 1949– . II. At issue (San Diego, Calif.)
HV5822.M38C58 2005
362.29'9—dc22
                                                                2004052289

Printed in the United States of America

Contents

Introduction

Raves—all-night parties featuring electronic music—originated in Europe in the early 1980s and quickly spread to England. By 1990 raves were becoming popular in the United States and could be found in most U.S. metropolitan areas. Raves have been linked to club drugs—particularly MDMA (Ecstasy)—almost from their initial appearance in the United States.

When raves came to America, Ecstasy immediately became part of the rave scene, creating considerable controversy. Brian Behlendorf, one of the original developers of the free Apache Web server and a fan of raves and rave culture, says,

> The subject of drugs at raves is very controversial. One wonders whether the rave scene would have been more easily accepted by the public had the presence of drugs not been so high. Of course, many others wonder how raves could have ever come about without them.

Many argue that music and drug use have always been connected, from the jazz clubs of the 1920s and 1930s to the rock concerts of the 1960s. Thus, many rave advocates maintain, raves and club drugs are the natural continuation of the music/drug link. Some researchers concur, suggesting that the hypnotic effect of the music and a youthful audience predisposed to drug use are an old combination at work in a new venue, and that the rave/club drug phenomenon is not unique.

According to researcher and writer Michael Walker, American raves started out as small, secretive gatherings and gradually became larger, more commercial events. Associated with a dance-oriented mix of amplified techno music controlled by a disc jockey, raves usually attract a youthful audience. Promoters who organize raves usually advertise them on Internet Web sites, post flyers locally, and depend on word of mouth to bring in crowds. Promoters are largely responsible for the safety of rave participants. They must select a safe venue that conforms to fire codes and has adequate emergency exits. In addition, large raves often have medical teams in attendance. The com-

4

bination of lack of air conditioning, long hours of dancing that contributes to fatigue and dehydration, and hyperthermia sometimes associated with Ecstasy use can lead to illnesses, even deaths. Cool-down rooms, air conditioned portions of the rave site, are often set aside so ravers can rest and avoid overheating from dancing or drug use.

In an effort to make raves as safe as possible, promoters often cooperate with DanceSafe, a national harm reduction organization that offers accurate information so that those who choose to use drugs can do so as safely as possible. Emanuel Sferios, a former social worker and founder of DanceSafe, argues, "It's not that there are good drugs and bad drugs, safe drugs and dangerous drugs. There are just drugs. All of them have inherent risk. People who aren't willing to abstain need factual, unbiased information about what the drugs do and how to avoid the risks." DanceSafe peer volunteers attend raves and provide literature about safe sex practices and the dangers of drug use; hand out free condoms, bottled water, and fruit; and offer to test Ecstasy for adulterating substances. DanceSafe counselors do a quick chemical test to determine if the sample the ravers have given them is only Ecstasy, if it has been mixed with another drug such as amphetamine, or if it is a capsule or pill containing table sugar or cornstarch. The counselors explain the results of the test to the ravers and then return their drugs to them. Sferios explains, "If we told kids we were planning to take their pills away, they'd never come around to read the [harm reduction] literature in the first place."

Many drug prohibitionists, however, are deeply concerned about raves and disagree with the concept of harm reduction. In an effort to eliminate drug use entirely, they have pushed for anti-rave legislation. The RAVE (Reducing Americans' Vulnerability to Ecstasy) Act of 2002, which sought to broaden a federal law originally aimed at crack houses, was defeated by opposition from the electronic music industry. The RAVE Act was renamed the Illicit Drug Anti-Proliferation Act of 2003, and in April of that year was passed as an attachment to the Amber Alert bill. This act holds business owners responsible for the crimes of their customers—specifically drug use. It allows the government to impose a quarter million dollar fine on business owners if drug use takes place on their property, even if they tried to stop it. Property owners, promoters, and event coordinators can face thousands of dollars in fines and face up to twenty years in prison if raves are held on their property. The American Civil Liberties

Union (ACLU) argues that the act threatens musical expression, free speech, and the right to dance. Further, it could harm those it was meant to help—ravers. According to the ACLU,

> Fear of massive fines and prison sentences will drive raves and other musical events underground and away from public health and safety regulations. If selling bottled water and offering "cooling off" rooms becomes proof that owners and promoters know drug use is occurring at their events, the . . . act will discourage harm-reduction measures, and the safety of our nation's youth will suffer.

The Drug Enforcement Administration (DEA), however, claims that the act will help fight drug trafficking and protect young people from Ecstasy and other club drugs. "Parents and teens often believe that events such as raves are safe and drug/alcohol-free. In reality, promoters often turn these events into havens of drug trafficking and use for their own illicit profit. This law is a helpful tool for law enforcement in addressing this problem." Rather than unfairly targeting innocent businesses, the DEA insists that "responsible enforcement of this law . . . will shield innocent businesses from criminal liability for incidental drug use by patrons while eliminating unlawful enterprises that lure young people into dangerous drug use."

While raves show no sign of decreasing in popularity despite this new law, it is difficult to know if they will become a permanent entertainment fixture or if they will disappear, not because of legislation or drug prohibition, but because young people will find a new venue for their music and drugs.

1

Recreational Use of Club Drugs Is Harmful

David M. McDowell

David M. McDowell is assistant clinical professor of psychiatry at Columbia University.

Club drugs such as MDMA (Ecstasy), ketamine, GHB, and Rohypnol are popular among teens who attend raves—all-night dance parties. While not considered as deadly or addictive as heroin or cocaine, club drugs are physiologically and psychologically harmful and may cause lasting damage. Ecstasy use can result in increased body temperature and blood pressure, dehydration, kidney failure, depression, and other mood changes. Research indicates that the drug can also cause long-term damage to the brain. Ketamine causes users to disconnect from the world, and GHB can cause death by overdose. Rohypnol, a sedative that causes short-term memory loss, has been implicated in many cases of date rape.

Much has been written about substance abuse within the youth culture. Some recent evidence indicates that the rates of such substances are rising. There are some illicit substances that are especially popular among young people. Methylenedioxymethamphetamine (MDMA), Ketamine, and Gamma Hydroxybutyrate (GHB) are unique compounds, differing in terms of their pharmacological properties and their phenomenological effects. They are particularly popular among young people who are part of the "rave" culture, but are used extensively by a wide variety of different people. Because of their use

David M. McDowell, testimony before the House Subcommittee on Crime, House Judiciary Committee, Washington, DC, June 15, 2000.

at various nightclubs, raves and other social events, they are widely known as "club drugs."

In recent years, the popularity of "club drugs" has been inextricably linked with the rise of the rave phenomenon. Raves first became popular in England during the late 1980s and have since spread to the United States and the rest of the world. In the early 1990s, raves were considered "the next big thing," a rising trend. Although their popularity has not grown dramatically, it has remained relatively constant. These events remain part of the popular youth culture, and are encountered in numerous venues. A mainstream example of this is "Groove," a movie about the rave culture, which opened commercially last week [June 2002] and was chosen as an official selection of the Sundance Film Festival.

At raves, groups of young people (typically in their teens) dance to rapid electronically synthesized music with no lyrics (techno). These events take place in unregulated and unlicensed locations such as stadiums, abandoned warehouses, and other surreptitious arenas. Since the early nineties, the venues have become increasingly mainstream. These drugs, along with marijuana and LSD, are extremely popular at these events. At some of these events, as many as 70% of rave participants are using Ecstasy, Ketamine, or GHB, along with other drugs such as marijuana and LSD.

Another event where these drugs are commonly used are at "circuit parties." Circuit parties are large-scale social events, which have become increasingly popular over the last decade. At these events, several thousand people, mostly (but not exclusively) young gay men, congregate in a dance club setting. Recently, they have become much larger, and spawned a worldwide industry, including a magazine called *Circuit Noize*, which is dedicated to issues related to circuit parties.

MDMA causes brain damage

MDMA [Ecstasy] has unique subjective and biochemical properties. Recreational use of MDMA has been illegal since it was made a Schedule I drug on July 1, 1985. Prior to that time, because it was not mentioned in the controlled substances act of 1970, its use was unregulated and therefore legal. In spite of its present illegal status, the popularity of MDMA has skyrocketed in the past several years. In the past several *months* it has become readily apparent that the trafficking of the drug, and its use, is far more widespread than once believed. This rise in usage has been particularly marked among adolescents, where MDMA usage is prevalent at raves, and other nightlife settings.

Research in mammals and non-human primates has shown that MDMA damages brain serotonin axons. These species share many characteristics with their human counterparts. The weight of scientific evidence indicates that Ecstasy does the same in humans. Research with MDMA in humans is logistically and scientifically difficult to accomplish, thus the evidence that MDMA is neurotoxic in humans comes indirectly from these studies. A number of recent research articles have demonstrated that individuals who use ecstasy, compared to matched controls who have not used MDMA, have decreased amounts of serotonin metabolites in their spinal fluid, and decreased serotonin activity as measured by brain imaging and cognitive deficits. The direct implication is that using MDMA does indeed damage neurons. This is particularly germane for individuals who may be prone to mental illness, because it is known that lower serotonin metabolite levels correspond with depression, impulsiveness, and suicide.

> *70% of rave participants are using Ecstasy, Ketamine, or GHB, along with other drugs such as marijuana and LSD.*

MDMA's appeal rests primarily on its psychological effect. It causes a dramatic and consistent feeling of attachment and connection. This feeling of connection is not necessarily to another individual, but rather, people who use the drug alone may feel "connected to" the larger world. Ecstasy is perhaps a misnomer, the LA dealer who coined the term wanted to call the drug "Empathy", but asked, "Who would know what that means?"

MDMA is not a new drug. Merck in Darmstadt, Germany first patented it in 1914. MDMA was probably first created as so many compounds were at that time, to serve for subsequent research. Except for a minor chemical modification in a patent in 1919, there is no other known historical record of MDMA until the 1950's. At that time, the United States Army experimented with MDMA, as well as with numerous other compounds. The resulting informational material was declassified and became available to the general public in the early 1970s. MDMA was apparently not used on humans at that time.

MDMA was probably first used by humans in the late 1960s. It was lionized as a recreational drug by free thinkers and "New Age Seekers," people who liked its property to induce feelings of well-being and connection. Given this capacity, a number of practitioners and researchers interested in insight-oriented psychotherapy believed it would be an ideal agent to enhance therapy. It was used extensively for this purpose, until it became illegal in 1985.

MDMA makes users docile

In the early 1980's, MDMA had an explosion in popularity. The drug's capacity to induce feelings of connection, as well as a psychomotor agitation, that can be pleasurably relieved by dancing, made it the ideal "party drug." In spite of widespread usage during the early 1980s, the drug did not attract much attention from law enforcement officials. This is not particularly surprising in that individuals on the drug tend to be complacent and docile.

Events in Texas, especially in the Dallas/Fort Worth area, changed this lack of notoriety. Until 1985, the drug was not scheduled or regulated and its use was legal. A distribution network in Texas began an aggressive marketing campaign and, for a time, the drug was available over the counter at bars, at convenience stores, and even through a toll-free number. This attracted the attention of then Texas Senator Lloyd Bentsen (the future vice presidential candidate, and Secretary of the Treasury). He petitioned the FDA [Food and Drug Administration], and the compound was placed on Schedule I on an emergency basis as of July 1, 1985. Originally, three hearings were scheduled to determine MDMA's permanent scheduling status. At that time, the compound's neurotoxicity was already an issue; as a result, MDMA was placed on Schedule I on a permanent basis. Schedule I refers to substances that have no therapeutic value, and which are considered to have high abuse potential. Clinical use is therefore prohibited, and because of the intense regulation of Schedule I compounds, research with MDMA is technically possible, but very difficult to execute.

The chemical synthesis of MDMA is relatively simple, and it is often made in illicit laboratories. In addition, it is often "cut" with other substances so the purity and dosage varies substantially. It currently sells in urban areas for about $25 to $30 per 125 mg tablet, which produces the sought after effect in most intermittent users.

> *Research in mammals and non-human primates has shown that MDMA damages brain serotonin axons.*

Tablets of MDMA are usually taken by mouth. Other methods of administration are much less popular, and virtually unheard of. The usual single dosage is between 100–150 mg. The effect of MDMA occurs in several stages. The initial stage begins with the onset of effect 20–40 minutes after ingestion and is experienced as a sudden, amphetamine-like "rush." Other effects, that simultaneously accompany the "rush," can be nausea, usually mild, but sometimes severe enough to cause vomiting, as well as the intense desire to defecate, known as a "disco dump."

The second, or "plateau stage," of drug effect lasts between three and six hours. Most users experience this feeling as a powerful connection to those around them; this may include the larger world. According to most users, this profound feeling of relatedness to the rest of the world is the reason to take the drug. In general, people on the drug appear to be less aggressive, and less impulsive than their non–drug using counterparts. Users also experience an altered perception of time and a decreased inclination to perform mental and physical tasks. Although the desire for sex can increase, the ability to achieve arousal and orgasm for both sexes is greatly diminished. It has thus been termed a sensual, not a sexual, drug. People on the drug also have mild feelings of restlessness, teeth grinding, jaw clenching, loss of appetite, sweating, hot flashes, tremor and "goose bumps." This array of physical effects and behaviors produced by MDMA is remarkably similar across mammalian species.

Depression and listlessness are common

The common after-effects can be pronounced, and may last 24 hours, or even longer. The most dramatic "hangover" effect is a sometimes-severe feeling of depression and listlessness. Users of MDMA can experience lethargy, anorexia, decreased motivation, sleepiness, depressed mood and fatigue. There are sometimes more severe after-effects. These include changes in thinking, convulsions, deregulated temperature control, changes in blood pressure, a racing heart rate, kidney failure, and even death.

There are numerous case reports of a single dose of MDMA precipitating severe psychiatric illness. MDMA does induce a range of depressive symptoms and anxiety in some individuals, and for that reason, people with depression and anxiety should be specifically cautioned about the dangers of using MDMA. Many of these reports represent single cases and there are often other potential explanations for these occurrences. Still, the growing number of such adverse events is cause for concern.

MDMA is a "dirty drug," because it affects a number of neurotransmitter systems, in particular, serotonin and dopamine-containing neurons. MDMA's primary mechanism of action is as an indirect serotonergic agonist. After being ingested, MDMA is taken up by the serotonin cell through an active channel where it causes the release of stored serotonin. The drug also blocks re-uptake of this neurotransmitter, contributing to its length of action. (It also inhibits further synthesis, but this effect probably does not contribute to the intoxicating effects. It may however, contribute to sustained feelings of depression reported by some users, and the diminished magnitude of subjective effects if the next dose is taken within a few days of the first.) The drug's effects and side effects including anorexia, psychomotor agitation, difficulty in achieving orgasm, and profound feelings of empathy, can all be explained as results of the flooding of the serotonin system.

> *Although the desire for sex [among Ecstasy users] can increase, the ability to achieve arousal and orgasm for both sexes is greatly diminished.*

Unlike other substances of abuse, where escalating dosage and frequency are common, people who use MDMA on a regular basis tend not to increase dosage as time goes on. Because the drug depletes serotonin stores and inhibits synthesis of new serotonin, subsequent doses produce a diminished "high," and a worsening of the drug's undesirable effects. Many users, who are at first enamored with the drug, eventually lose interest, usually citing the substantial side effects. It is rare, although certainly possible, to find someone who uses the drug very often (more than once per week) over the course of years. There is an adage on college campuses about Ecstasy that captures this phenomenon: "freshmen love it, sophomores like it, juniors are ambivalent, and seniors are afraid of it." Those who do continue to use the drug over longer periods of time usually tend to use the drug only periodically. It is therefore reserved for "special occasions." Many young people report "saving" their Ecstasy use for special occasions, especially for important raves, or parties.

> *There are numerous case reports of a single dose of MDMA precipitating severe psychiatric illness.*

In the early and mid 1990s, there was a rash of deaths associated with the use of MDMA. These deaths mostly occurred at raves and appear to be similar to certain features of both the "Serotonin Syndrome" and the Neuroleptic Malignant Syndrome. The Serotonin Syndrome is a clinical phenomenon that occurs with an excess of the neurotransmitter serotonin and is characterized by confusion, restlessness, increased temperature, sweating, increased reflexes, diarrhea, and muscle twitches. The Neuroleptic Malignant Syndrome (NMS) is more often associated with the use of anti-psychotic medicine (dopamine blockers) and dehydration, and its symptoms consist of confusion, increased temperature, elevated levels of muscle enzymes, and autonomic dysfunction. Both syndromes exist on a spectrum of severity, but in their most severe form they are life threatening, and may lead to death.

Dehydration may lead to death

Raves are often held in hot, crowded conditions. Some clubs turned off their water supplies in an effort to maximize profits by selling bottled water. The hot, crowded conditions, physical exertion, and subsequent dehydration, combined with the drug effects, contributed to the deaths. After these incidents, the English government mandated an open water supply at all clubs; deaths of this kind appear to have since diminished, though they do still occur. In recent years, one of the principal aims of harm reduction efforts, in Europe and the United States, aimed at young people who take the drug, is to remind them that if they are going to take the drug, they must keep well hydrated.

> ***It is exceedingly easy to overdose from GHB; the intoxicating dose and the lethal dose are quite similar.*"**

Although rare, there have been anecdotal reports of MDMA causing Post Hallucinogenic Perception Disorder. This disorder is a prolonged re-experience of the perceptual distortion produced during the MDMA "high." Post Hallucinogenic Perceptual Disorder is more commonly associated with LSD ingestion, and can last for months, even years. Although symptoms tend to diminish over time, there are no effective treatments for this disorder.

In laboratory animals, the ingestion of MDMA causes a decrease in the serum and spinal fluid levels of serotonin metabolites in a dose-dependent fashion and damages brain serotonin neurons. In non-human primates, the neurotoxic dose approximates the recreational dose taken by humans. Like its close structural relative MDA [Methylenedioxyamphetamine], MDMA has been found to damage serotonin neurons in all animal species tested to date.

Unequivocal data demonstrating that similar changes occur in the human brain do not yet exist, but the indirect clinical evidence is disconcerting. MDMA users have significantly less serotonin metabolites in their spinal fluid than matched controls. Clear deficits and major neurotoxicity appear to be related to total cumulative dose in animals. In addition, MDMA produces a 30–35% drop in serotonin metabolism in humans. It is possible that even one dose of MDMA may cause lasting damage to the serotonin system. Furthermore, such damage might only become apparent with time, or under conditions of stress. Users with no initial complications may manifest problems over time.

There have been reports of individuals with lasting neuropsychiatric disturbances after MDMA use and it warrants particular caution, because the axonal destruction, though apparent on sophisticated cognitive testing, may not be readily apparent for many years after use. However, there is a growing number of recent studies demonstrating that individuals who currently use Ecstasy *do* have cognitive changes compared to those who have never taken the drug. The use of Ecstasy may affect the reserves of the serotonin system by severely diminishing them. As individuals age, they may not have the same level of stores of functional serotonin cells once available. This results in low serotonin levels, which are associated with such serious consequences as depression, violence, and suicide.

The clinical impact of serotonergic damage is not clear, since some animal data suggest that even significant destruction of serotonin neurons leads to little functional impairment. Recent studies in humans, using matched controls of people who have not ever taken MDMA, have demonstrated that the use of the drug does have an impact on memory, and a number of other cognitive functions. The drug's probable neurotoxicity is the most significant concern about its use.

Club drugs also consist of a number of other substances of abuse. Among these are Ketamine ("special K"), rohypnol ("roofies") and GHB—gamma-hydroxybutyrate ("liquid Ecstasy"); in Britain, as GBH ("grievous bodily harm"). Ketamine is a disassociative anesthetic, and causes people to appear disconnected from the world. GHB is prized for its ability to relax and cause stimulation at the same time. It is exceedingly easy to overdose from GHB; the intoxicating dose and the lethal dose are quite similar. Rohypnol is a short acting benzodiazepine that is better known as "the date rape drug," as it causes short-term memory loss in people who use it, and can be surreptitiously dropped into an unsuspecting victim's drink.

The substances discussed above are used at raves, and at clubs, often in combination, and often by very young people. This is serious cause for concern for several reasons. Among these reasons are that the younger a person begins using drugs, and the more often, the more likely he or she will progress to having a serious drug problem. It is understandable why so many adolescents may find raves, and the club drugs used there, so appealing. Ecstasy, in particular, is alluring and seductive. But as stated above, there is a darker side to this story. It is likely that permanent damage to the serotonin system is occurring in individuals who use Ecstasy and other club drugs. The extent and consequences of this damage may not become apparent for decades.

2

Recreational Use of Ecstasy May Cause Long-Term Brain Damage

Brendon P. Boot, Iain S. McGregor, and Wayne Hall

Brendon P. Boot is a member of the faculty of medicine at the University of Sydney and a researcher at the National Drug and Alcohol Research Centre, University of New South Wales, Sydney, Australia. Iain S. McGregor is a member of the Department of Psychology at the University of Sydney. Wayne Hall is a researcher at the National Drug and Alcohol Research Centre, University of New South Wales, Sydney, Australia.

Because controlled research on MDMA's effects on humans is currently forbidden, scientists must rely primarily on animal tests and observational studies of recreational users to determine the neurological damage the drug can cause. Their findings indicate that MDMA, also called Ecstasy, can cause dehydration, hyperthermia, and depression as well as long-term cognitive, behavioral, and emotional problems.

MDMA (3,4-methylenedioxymethamphetamine) is an amphetamine analogue that produces euphoric and stimulant effects and a feeling of closeness towards others. For more than a decade, MDMA (colloquially known as "Ecstasy" or "E")

Brendon P. Boot, Iain S. McGregor, and Wayne Hall, "MDMA (Ecstasy) Neurotoxicity: Assessing and Communicating the Risks," *The Lancet*, vol. 355, May 20, 2000. Copyright © 2000 by Elsevier Science Publishers. Reproduced by permission.

has been widely used by young adults as a dance-party drug.

The usual recreational oral dose is 1–2 tablets (each containing about 60–120 mg of MDMA) a standard oral dose of 0.75–4.00 mg per kg in 60–80 kg people. MDMA is typically used once fortnightly [once every two weeks] or less because tolerance to the effects of MDMA develops rapidly. More frequent use requires larger doses to achieve the desired effects, but this increases the prevalence of unpleasant side-effects.

> *“ The perceived safety of MDMA is at odds with animal evidence of MDMA neurotoxicity. ”*

A number of deaths have occurred as a result of malignant hyperthermia or idiosyncractic reactions to the drug, but these have been rare. MDMA is perceived by many users to be a safe drug. Few report the craving associated with opiates or cocaine and most MDMA users are aware of only mild and transient disruptions of functioning. The perceived safety of MDMA is at odds with animal evidence of MDMA neurotoxicity, an increasing prevalence of hazardous patterns of use among recreational MDMA users, and emerging evidence of neurotoxicity among heavier MDMA users.

MDMA neurotoxicity in primates

MDMA administration in rodents and non-human primates produces large and possibly permanent damage to axons and axon terminal fibres containing 5-hydroxytryptamine (5-HT, serotonin). Long-term reductions in the density of 5-HT axons are most evident in the cortex, hippocampus, and striatum. Other markers of brain 5-HT function, including the density of 5-HT uptake sites and the concentration of the 5-HT metabolite 5-hydroxyindoleacetic acid (5-HIAA), are similarly reduced. The mechanism underlying this neurotoxicity has not yet been determined, although a role for MDMA-induced hyperthermia and free-radical formation is likely. Decreases in the density of brain 5-HT axons have been seen in squirrel monkeys more than 7 years after MDMA administration. Some regrowth of axons occurs, but this is abnormal and incomplete.

Most of these animal studies have administered 5 mg per

kg of MDMA twice daily for four consecutive days, which is much higher and more frequent dosing than is typical in human users. Moreover, in animal studies MDMA is often injected subcutaneously, which in monkeys is two to three times more neurotoxic than the oral route preferred by human users. Because of these differences in dose and route of administration, proponents of recreational MDMA use have argued that this animal evidence has little relevance to human users. This ignores the well-established principles of interspecies dosage scaling which indicate that larger animals are more susceptible to the toxic effects of a given dose of a drug than smaller animals. In the case of MDMA, primates are more susceptible to MDMA neurotoxicity than rats, which in turn are more susceptible than mice.

Surveys suggest that a substantial minority of recreational MDMA users use the drug in a way that increases the risk of 5-HT neurotoxicity. First, one in six of a sample of 329 Australian users had injected MDMA at some time. Second, 42% had used MDMA for 48 [hours] or more at least once in the past 6 months. Third, the intake of multiple tablets in a single-use episode may be increasing. Finally, MDMA is often used in environments that are hot and crowded with limited access to drinking water, increasing the risk of hyperthermia, which exacerbates MDMA neurotoxicity in rats.

Evidence of neurotoxicity in MDMA users

Suggestive evidence of neurotoxicity in human MDMA users has emerged during the past decade. Decreased concentrations of 5-HIAA in the cerebrospinal fluid of MDMA users have been noted in several studies. Studies measuring the prolactin response to an L-tryptophan, M-chlorophenylpiperazine, or D-fenfluramine challenge in MDMA users have for the most part suggested a blunted neuroendocrine response to serotonergic agonists.

Two brain-imaging studies have provided more compelling evidence of MDMA neurotoxicity. [U.D.] McCann and colleagues reported reduced binding of the radioligand McN-5652 in several brain regions in MDMA users, indicating a reduced density of 5-HT uptake sites. The same research group showed reductions in axon densities in baboons at necropsy with similarly decreased McN-5652 binding following neurotoxic doses of MDMA.

Critics have argued that low 5-HT function may be a cause

rather than an effect of MDMA use because low concentrations of 5-HT have been linked to impulsivity and sensation seeking in humans. It is therefore notable that [D.M.] Semple and colleagues have shown a decreased density of 5-HT uptake sites in the brains of heavy MDMA users compared with controls who were well matched for alcohol, tobacco, and cannabis use. Regional differences in 5-HT transporter density were far fewer in this study than in the study of McCann and colleagues, possibly because the radioligand used by Semple and colleagues had higher non-specific binding.

Two studies have suggested other alterations in the brains of MDMA users. One reported a reduction in brain glucose metabolism in the left hippocampus of users, but this was the only significant difference seen in 14 brain regions assessed. The other study showed correlations between extent of MDMA use and indices of electroencephalogram (EEG) power and coherence. The EEG patterns of the heavier MDMA users were similar to those seen with ageing and dementia.

The consequences of MDMA damage

If MDMA does damage 5-HT systems in humans, what functional consequences should we expect? Initial studies suggested only moderate behavioural or cognitive deficits in laboratory animals given neurotoxic doses of MDMA. Some research suggesting 5-HT neurotoxicity in human MDMA users has also found an absence of symptoms. Nonetheless, there have been many case reports of neuropsychiatric sequelae after MDMA use, and an increasing number of controlled studies suggest cognitive, behavioural, and emotional problems in MDMA users.

Impulsivity—[P.] Soubrie has suggested that 5-HT may have a central role in behavioural inhibition. Rats with 5-HT damage are impulsive, insensitive to punishment, and hyperactive in the face of novelty. Human beings with low concentrations of 5-HIAA in cerebrospinal fluid have exhibited violent, impulsive, alcoholic, and criminal behaviour. One report has shown that MDMA users are more impulsive than matched polydrug-using controls on a laboratory behavioural measure but there are also contradictory results.

Depression—Depressed patients and successful suicides show various abnormal indices of 5-HT function. At least two studies have now documented a transient depression of mood in the days following MDMA use. This depression seems to have lifted by 1 week after MDMA use. Such a pattern of mood change is consistent with MDMA's short-term effects on the concentrations of brain 5-HT. A more persistent lowering of mood is suggested by the high prevalence of depressive symptoms in a sample of Australian MDMA users. The prevalence of irritability, depression, and sleep disturbances was related to frequency of MDMA use, reported dose of MDMA, binge use of MDMA, and the number of other drugs used to manage the after-effects of MDMA use. These results are consistent with other findings from Italy.

> // *Surveys suggest that a substantial minority of recreational MDMA users use the drug in a way that increases the risk of . . . neurotoxicity.* //

Cognitive dysfunction—Serotonergic damage may adversely affect memory and higher cognitive function. The hippocampal formation receives a dense 5-HT innervation that may be particularly vulnerable to MDMA's neurotoxic effects. One study found profound deficits in working memory in rats exposed to high doses of MDMA.

Data now also indicate an acute disruptive effect of MDMA on short-term memory in human beings, as well as a longer term impairment in memory and cognition. Both verbal and visual memory impairments have been noted in long-term users tested in the drug-free state. One study that shows memory deficits in MDMA users compared with a control group of polydrug users who have not used MDMA is particularly compelling. Deficits have also been seen in tests of logical reasoning and serial addition.

Continued research

Only a prospective study of 5-HT function in MDMA-naive individuals that are randomly assigned to MDMA or placebo conditions could definitively show that recreational MDMA use was neurotoxic in human beings. For ethical, political, and legal reasons such a study is unlikely to ever be done. Instead, we have to rely upon evidence from observational studies of recreational MDMA users. These need to include large samples of a broad range of MDMA users to assess the link between MDMA use and indicators of neurotoxicity. The use of appropriately matched control groups is critical in such studies. It is important to find out whether suggestive evidence of neurotoxic effects in the heavy MDMA users tested to date also occur in less frequent users. Some have argued that even a single moderate oral dose of MDMA may be neurotoxic in human beings although this claim is controversial and difficult to verify on the basis of current evidence. Future studies should specifically address this important issue.

> *An increasing number of controlled studies suggest cognitive, behavioural, and emotional problems in MDMA users.*

Other emerging diseases associated with long-term MDMA use also need to be better described. These include: cardiac dysfunction, eating disorders, thermoregulatory deficits, sleep abnormalities, and congenital defects in babies exposed to MDMA in utero. Verification of a reported risk of clinical depression and suicide in MDMA users is a priority. MDMA users with memory dysfunction should be studied prospectively to find out whether dysfunction resolves with abstinence or increases with age. PET [Positron Emission Tomography] and other imaging studies might be combined with neuropsychological assessment to study links between decreases in 5-HT uptake sites in specific brain regions and memory loss.

An opportunity should be taken to investigate the human neurotoxicity of fenetylline (fenfluoramine) and dexfenetylline (dexfenfluramine), both of which were recently withdrawn from the market. These rugs cause 5-HT neurotoxicity in laboratory animals that is very similar to that seen with MDMA. More than 50 million people have been prescribed these drugs worldwide, so studies of possible functional deficits in these people may help to define the risks of MDMA use.

There are also anecdotal reports that some MDMA users are combining MDMA with selective serotonin reuptake inhibitor (SSRI) drugs such as fluoxetine to dampen the dysphoria experienced after MDMA use. Fluoxetine, when administered before or soon after MDMA, provides some protection against neurotoxicity in animals but there are also concerns that it could potentiate acute toxic effects of the MDMA in susceptible individuals. The interaction between SSRIs and MDMA and between MDMA and other widely used illicit drugs should be more thoroughly investigated.

Health education

The consistency of the clinical, epidemiological, and neurological studies reviewed strongly suggests that MDMA can produce neurotoxic effects in some recreational users. Those individuals who are at greatest risk are those who use two or more street doses of MDMA at a time, those who use the drug fortnightly or more frequently, those who inject MDMA, and those who use MDMA for 24 [hours] or more.

Current and potential users of MDMA need to be told about these risks by education delivered by peers in the dance-party milieu and through the media used by members of this subculture (eg, videos and the internet). Peer-based education of injecting drug users about the risks of infectious disease from equipment sharing, in combination with needle and syringe programmes, has substantially changed risk behaviour in this population. A similar approach may also be successful among MDMA users who are better educated and less socially disadvantaged than injecting drug users.

A non-alarmist and accurate portrayal of the evidence is required if it is to receive the support of influential individuals in the MDMA-using subculture. Such an education campaign should acknowledge uncertainties about the risks of occasional use of "low" doses of MDMA while emphasising the risks that heavier and more frequent MDMA users probably face. It could also include suggestions on how to minimise any neurotoxic effects (such as avoidance of hyperthermia) and the risks of bingeing and injecting MDMA should be highlighted. Finally, MDMA users need to be warned that neurotoxic effects may occur in the absence of subjectively noticeable symptoms.

3

The Harmfulness of Ecstasy Has Been Exaggerated

Rick Doblin

Rick Doblin is founder and president of the Multidisciplinary Association for Psychedelic Studies (MAPS), a research and educational organization that sponsors clinical studies designed to obtain approval from the Food and Drug Administration (FDA) for the use of MDMA (Ecstasy) as a prescription medicine.

Flawed research has been conducted to purposely mislead the public and scientific community regarding the risks of using Ecstasy. Exaggerating the dangers of using Ecstasy has successfully halted research into the possible therapeutic uses of the drug. Further, overstating the drug's harmfulness has led to excessive antirave legislation and increased criminal penalties for using it. The harmful effects of recreational use of Ecstasy can be mitigated by the judicious use of effective harm reduction techniques, such as adequate hydration and prevention of overheating. Only scientifically accurate, politically unbiased research into the effects of the drug on the human brain will provide answers as to the true risks and benefits of Ecstasy.

The Ricaurte et al. retraction of their article claiming that MDMA [Ecstasy] causes Parkinson's, originally published in *Science* in September 2002 and retracted in September 2003, has created a unique opportunity for an interwoven series of chal-

23

lenges to the perception that any use of MDMA is exceptionally risky and dangerous. This perception has been created in the minds of the general public, regulators and lawmakers by NIDA/ONDCP/DEA/[National Institute on Drug Abuse/Office of National Drug Control Policy/Drug Enforcement Administration] Partnership for a Drug-Free America. According to this dominant but misleading view, even a single or a few uses can cause significant long-term brain damage with important deleterious functional consequences. From a scientific perspective, however, claims about the negative effects of MDMA on dopamine, serotonin and cerebral blood flow, by Drs. [George M.] Ricaurte, and [Unal D.] McCann and Dr. Alan Leshner, ex-Director of the National Institute on Drug Abuse, respectively, have either been retracted, shown to contain major methodological flaws, or are clearly misleading.

> *According to this dominant but misleading view, even a single or a few uses can cause significant long-term brain damage.*

The controversy surrounding the retraction provides some relatively easy ways to explain how scientific information has been misleadingly presented by grant-addicted scientists and prohibitionists and has facilitated the ramping up of the penalties against the non-medical use of MDMA, the efforts to shut down the rave movement, and the pressure to prevent research into the therapeutic uses of MDMA-assisted psychotherapy. Fortunately, the new NIDA Director Dr. Nora Volkow seems likely to live up to a statement she made in an August 19, 2003, *New York Times* interview, in which she said "If you want to be a scientist, you cannot allow politics to get in the way of your objectivity."

Erroneous findings

Ricaurte/McCann now acknowledge that their evidence about MDMA damaging dopamine neurons was erroneous (Ricaurte et al. 2003) and was based on the mistaken administration to their primates of methamphetamine instead of MDMA, supposedly due to mislabeled 10 gram bottles of MDMA and methamphetamine which arrived from the same provider in the same package. A September 18, 2003 editorial in *Nature* asked NIDA Director Nora Volkow to conduct a "thorough public review" of the circumstances and participant's roles in one of the more bizzare episodes in the history of drug research. The *Nature* editorial also accused former NIDA Director Leshner, now Executive Director of the American Association for the Advancement of Science (AAAS), which publishes *Science*, of "pander[ing] to the Bush administration's jihad against recreational drug use." The accusation was based in part on his hyperbolic statements in the press release that *Science* issued to draw attention to the original article, in which he said, "Using Ecstasy is like playing Russian roulette with your brain function." A September 18, 2003 news report in *The Scientist* mentions that Ricaurte/McCann have retracted a second paper and reports that two senior British scientists have demanded that *Science* investigate its review of the original article and release the comments of the peer reviewers.

An October 14, 2003 article in *Lancet Neurology* reports that MAPS [Multidisciplinary Association for Psychedelic Studies] has filed a FOIA [Freedom of Information Act] request with NIDA seeking more data on Ricaurte/McCann's other recent NIDA-funded research in order to determine whether additional studies need to be retracted. To date, Ricaurte et al. have accounted for less than 2¼ grams of the 10 grams of methamphetamine that was contained in the original bottle mislabeled MDMA, all of which was used in research before the mislabeling was discovered. No accounting has yet been made of which studies used the MDMA from the bottle mislabeled methamphetamine.

> *If you want to be a scientist, you cannot allow politics to get in the way of your objectivity.*

Since MAPS is seeking to conduct FDA [Food and Drug Administration]-approved research in which MDMA is administered to human subjects, our FOIA request also seeks the release of more details about the design and results of Dr. Ricaurte and McCann's subsequent studies that they mention in their retraction, in which they administered genuine MDMA to primates, both orally and by injection, and found no evidence of dopaminergic neurotoxicity. These studies can provide data that bears directly on the estimation of the risk of dopaminergic neurotoxicity to subjects in the human research that MAPS is seeking to conduct.

Anti-Ecstasy bias

Ricaurte/McCann's anti-Ecstasy bias is now more clearly visible. In their original *Science* paper with its surprising results, the authors ignored three published human studies showing no effect of MDMA on dopamine, claimed that they administered the equivalent of a "common recreational dose regime" despite a reported 20% mortality rate in their primates (later modified to a 13.3% death rate when Ricaurte et al. admitted that they actually used 5 more animals than they reported to gather the data for their original *Science* article), and ignored their own research showing that oral administration of MDMA is less neurotoxic than the injection of MDMA. These and other criticisms of the original study were published in *Science* in a letter written by the MAPS MDMA/PTSD [Posttraumatic Stress Disorder] research team.

Ricaurte et al.'s retraction letter itself provides further evidence of their anti-Ecstasy bias. In the retraction letter, Drs. Ricaurte and McCann still claim that doses of MDMA used by some humans could cause dopaminergic neurotoxicity and Parkinson's, based on exceedingly flimsy evidence.

Ironically, recent animal research has been published showing that MDMA, when administered in combination with L-Dopa, actually helps reduce dyskinesias, painful symptoms of Parkinson's.

> *MDMA caused no persisting long-term differences in cerebral blood flow as compared to the non-MDMA using controls.*

McCann et al.'s evidence from their PET [Positron Emission Tomography] studies in Ecstasy users on which they based their claims that MDMA causes massive reductions in serotonin, published in the *Lancet*, are now generally considered to be based on methodologically flawed data. Basically, the values for the serotonin transporter levels in McCann's control group are so spread out, with some control subjects having 35 times more serotonin transporters than others, as to be biologically implausible. To deal with this variation, McCann et al. log transformed their data, something no other PET researchers have needed to do. Subsequent studies by other researchers using the same PET technique generated control values similar to McCann's Ecstasy users. A much larger and better controlled study, published in the *Journal of Nuclear Medicine*, with 117 subjects as compared to McCann's 29, found that former users of Ecstasy, who had consumed an average of 799 doses and had abstained for about 18 months, had serotonin levels identical to that of the control subjects. [R.] Buchert et al. found that current users of Ecstasy, with an average exposure of 827 doses, showed no reductions in some brain regions and only minimal reductions (4–6%) in two other brain regions, unlikely to be of even temporary clinical significance.

A bogus ad campaign

The data from McCann et al.'s *Lancet* paper formed the basis of NIDA's major anti-Ecstasy educational campaign, the Plain Brain/Brain After Ecstasy image. NIDA had this image printed on hundreds of thousands of cards distributed in bars and restaurants across the United States, used the image in NIDA publications and websites, and encouraged its use in media reports, all part of its now-abandoned $42 million "club drugs" campaign. This image wasn't even an accurate representation of the data in the *Lancet* article if that data had actually been valid. NIDA used images chosen for dramatic effect comparing subjects from the extremes of the MDMA and control groups rather than from the subjects scoring closest to the median, using some normal individual variability to exaggerate the evidence of MDMA neurotoxicity. NIDA has now withdrawn this educational campaign and even told the Peter Jennings' Ecstasy documentary team that it couldn't locate a copy of the image!

From another perspective, NIDA's anti-Ecstasy educational campaign, and Dr. Leshner's other efforts to pander to the Bush and Clinton administrations' jihad against recreational drug use, have been wildly successful. A simple chart showing the annual increases provided by Congress to NIDA's budget during the tenure of Dr. Leshner reveals the short-term dividends of exaggerating the risks of MDMA and other illicit drugs in support of prohibitionist policies.

Testimony that then-NIDA Director Alan Leshner gave on July 30, 2001 to the Senate Subcommittee on Government Affairs, illustrated with a large poster purporting to show that MDMA negatively affects (reduces) cerebral blood flow, was clearly misleading. The poster showed a healthy-looking brain with what was represented as normal cerebral blood flow, with this image labeled "Baseline." For comparison purposes, the poster also contained a second brain scan image of the same subject with reduced cerebral blood flow. This image was labeled "Two weeks post-MDMA." What Leshner didn't tell the Senators is that the scans were drawn from a study that showed no difference between Ecstasy users and controls in cerebral blood flow.

> *Ever since MDMA was criminalized . . . exaggerated risk estimates have played an essential role in preventing research into the therapeutic uses of MDMA.*

The images Leshner used in his Senate testimony came from one of the subset of the Ecstasy users in the larger study who participated in Dr. [Charles] Grob's Phase I MDMA safety study. These 10 subjects were scanned at baseline, like the other 11 Ecstasy-using subjects in Dr. [L.] Chang's research. They were then scanned again after receiving two doses of MDMA administered in the context of Dr. Grob's study, at time points ranging from two weeks to 2–3 months after the last dose of MDMA. Subjects scanned two weeks after MDMA showed a temporary reduction in cerebral blood flow while subjects scanned from 2–3 months after MDMA showed a return to baseline. The impression Leshner left the Senators was that MDMA caused permanent changes in cerebral blood flow when the changes were both temporary and of no clinical consequence.

Ironically, Leshner didn't realize that in order to participate in the Phase I study and receive MDMA, FDA required subjects to have already had substantial exposure to MDMA. On average, the subjects in Dr. Chang's study had an exposure to MDMA of 211 times. Thus, the healthy-looking brain that Leshner showed to the Senators to contrast with the image of the same brain two weeks post-MDMA was actually the brain of a heavy MDMA user at baseline! If he had fully understood the science underlying the images he showed to the Senator, Leshner should have reported that the baseline image dramatically illustrated that MDMA caused no persisting long-term differences in cerebral blood flow as compared to the non-MDMA using controls. Instead, he used the image to convey an impression of the dangers of MDMA at odds with what the study actually demonstrated.

No holes

Frightening and disturbing images of the brain of an MDMA user that showed explicit holes in the brain that were claimed to have been caused by MDMA have been shown on an MTV special documentary about Ecstasy, as well as on an Oprah Winfrey show. These images were graphically manipulated to represent areas of lower cerebral blood flow as holes and are completely fraudulent. According to a March 2001 educational program about drugs aimed at young people that NIDA helped create, Alan Leshner stated, "We've heard people talk about Ecstasy causing holes in the brain and of course that's a bit of an exaggeration, but there is a core truth to it." We should be appalled, but not surprised, at the fact that the young woman whose brain scan image was manipulated has been working for several years at the Partnership for a Drug-Free America, miseducating other young people about the dangers of MDMA (her choice of employment, perhaps, reflecting the only genuine signs of brain damage).

> *The risks of MDMA-related brain damage have been exaggerated, in yet another . . . example of science being twisted to suit political ends.*

Ever since MDMA was criminalized in the United States in 1985, exaggerated risk estimates have played an essential role in preventing research into the therapeutic uses of MDMA. In 1985, the FDA even refused to permit researchers to administer MDMA-assisted psychotherapy to a dying cancer patient who had experienced no significant side effects and had obtained relief from pain, both physical and emotional, through the use of such therapy that he had received prior to MDMA being made illegal. An FDA official wrote that even dying subjects deserved to be protected by US law from the potential damaging effects of MDMA neurotoxicity. In this case, it didn't matter that the damage was hypothetical, the benefits were real, and the patient was willing to accept the consequences of participating in the research.

> *The risks that MDMA does present can be mitigated to a large extent by the wise use of harm reduction efforts.*

In 1999, after human research with MDMA had begun in Switzerland, a group of Dutch researchers tried to stop Swiss researcher Dr. Franz Vollenweider from conducting basic safety studies by claiming in a letter to the journal *Neuropsychopharmacology* that Dr. Vollenweider was engaging in unethical research. Their rationale was that Dr. Vollenweider was administering MDMA to MDMA-naive subjects, a design that Dr. Vollenweider considered useful to obtain the clearest evidence of the effects of MDMA but that [researcher H.S.] Gijsman considered too risky due to the dangers of MDMA neurotoxicity. A debate took place in a series of letters published in *Neuropsychopharmacology*. Dr. Vollenweider defended his research and risk estimates. Courageously, the editors disagreed with Gijsman and supported Dr. Vollenweider's research. Two years later, Drs. McCann and Ricaurte entered the discussion to raise the issue of the dangers of MDMA neurotoxicity from even a single dose but were rebutted by Dr. Vollenweider and again by the editors.

Sadly, the world's only fully-approved MDMA psychotherapy study was successfully halted for political reasons, with efforts to restart the study complicated by Dr. Ricaurte. In 2000, in Madrid, Spain, Jose Carlos Bouso, with the support of MAPS, was able to obtain all the necessary federal and local permissions to start the world's first legally-approved controlled study into any therapeutic use of MDMA. The study was designed as a double-blind, placebo-controlled, dose-response pilot study into the use of MDMA-assisted psychotherapy in the treatment of women survivors of sexual assault with chronic, treatment-resistant posttraumatic stress disorder (PTSD). By April 2002, six subjects had been enrolled in the study without any complications. On May 6, 2002, favorable media coverage of the study appeared in prominent Spanish media. On May 13, 2002, as a result of pressure from the Madrid Anti-Drug Authority, the Manager of the Hospital Psiquiatrico de Madrid sent a letter saying that he wouldn't let the experimenters use the facilities of the Hospital anymore. In October 2002, just one week after Ricaurte's paper in *Science* came out, the research team's struggles to resume the study were significantly complicated by the appearance in Madrid of Dr. Ricaurte, who gave a highly-publicized talk about his MDMA/Parkinson's findings at the invitation of the Spanish Anti-Drug Agency. Additional talks by Dr. Ricaurte in Spain in April, June and July 2003, further reinforced both the scientific and popular perception in Spain of the dangerousness of even a few doses of MDMA. . . .

The struggle for government approval

MAPS has now worked for 17 years, since it was founded in 1986, to sponsor FDA-approved research investigating the therapeutic uses of MDMA. From 1986 to 1992, concerns over the risks of MDMA neurotoxicity were used to justify FDA refusals to approve any research in which MDMA was to be administered to human subjects. Starting in 1992, after a change in personnel and policy, FDA approved three basic safety studies with MDMA. The evidence from these studies, as well as from research conducted abroad, eventually persuaded the FDA that the risk/benefit ratio of MDMA was favorable in certain patient populations. As a result, in November 2001, the FDA approved a MAPS-sponsored pilot study into the use of MDMA-assisted psychotherapy in treatment-resistant PTSD subjects.

The controversy over the neurotoxic risks of MDMA, and over its widespread recreational use, made it exceptionally difficult for MAPS to obtain Institutional Review Board (IRB) approval for our study of the use of MDMA-assisted psychotherapy in subjects with chronic, treatment-resistant posttraumatic stress disorder (PTSD). Once IRB approved the study, then two months later revoked approval after an IRB official who wasn't comfortable with the approval of MDMA psychotherapy research spoke to Dr. Una McCann and two other researchers. The other two researchers actually supported the study (one initially and the other after MAPS agreed to add some language to the informed consent form), but Dr. McCann and Dr. Ricaurte refrained from doing so. The IRB refused to review the scientific evidence and made a policy decision to return the fee that MAPS paid for the review. Five other IRBs refused to even accept the protocol for review and one that did accept it finally tabled the review, after spending months formally reviewing the study before making it clear, through unreasonable demands, that the committee did not feel comfortable approving it. After diligent and persistent work, MAPS managed to obtain IRB approval in September 2003.

However, the study is still not fully approved. Research can start only after the principal investigator, Dr. Michael Mithoefer, receives a Schedule I license from the DEA so that he can legally possess and administer the total of 3 grams of MDMA that will be given to the subjects in the study (each MDMA subject in the MDMA group will receive two oral doses of 125 mgs each, three to five weeks apart). Dr. Mithoefer submitted his application to DEA for a Schedule I license over 17 months ago, with a decision from DEA still pending. On October 28, 2003 South Carolina DEA agents and officials from the South Carolina Department of Health and Environmental Control (DHEC) finally inspected Dr. Mithoefer's facility. They examined the DEA-required safe bolted to the concrete floor, the alarm system and the MDMA tracking procedures, in order to ensure that the 3.5 grams of MDMA will be protected from diversion to non-research uses. On November 12, 2003, Dr. Mithoefer received his Schedule I research registration (R1) from the DHEC. We expect that sometime soon DEA will issue Dr. Mithoefer his Schedule I license so that we can start MDMA psychotherapy research after more than 18 years of struggle.[1] (MDMA was criminalized in 1985 on an emergency basis, justified in part based on Dr. Ricaurte's research in rats showing that MDA, a drug related to MDMA, caused reductions in serotonin at some doses.)

The above review isn't meant to build a case that MDMA is harmless, or completely benign. MDMA has its risks, some of which can be fatal, like hyperthermia, a very rare occurrence that results from overheating, most often due to prolonged ex-

---

1. In March 2004 the DEA issued Dr. Mithoefer's Schedule I registration, clearing the way for him to immediately begin the first government-approved study of MDMA.

ercise and inadequate fluid replacement. The effects of heavy Ecstasy use on neurocognitive functioning is still being researched, with some well-designed studies showing that heavy MDMA users perform worse on some neurocognitive tests. Whether this is due to MDMA remains to be determined. What the above review is trying to communicate is that the risks of MDMA-related brain damage have been exaggerated, in yet another historical example of science being twisted to suit political ends. The risks that MDMA does present can be mitigated to a large extent by the wise use of harm reduction efforts. Unfortunately, the anti-rave legislation that Congress passed under the false assumption that MDMA caused unusually powerful brain damage after only a few doses perversely empowers police and prosecutors to use harm reduction efforts as a legal weapon against promoters and venue owners.

For almost two decades, MDMA research has been primarily focused on neurotoxicity research into the risks of MDMA, with MDMA psychotherapy research essentially forbidden. Perhaps the tide is turning and the next two decades will see a more balanced focus on research into both the potential risks and benefits of MDMA, with a variety of social, legal structures eventually to be created that will minimize the potential harms of MDMA and maximize its benefits. If we will it, it need not remain a dream.

4

Scientists Disagree on the Long-Term Effects of Ecstasy Use

David Concar

David Concar writes for the New Scientist *and other science publications.*

Researchers do not agree on the harmfulness of Ecstasy use. The short-term harms associated with using the drug, including heat stroke and depression, are well documented, but the occurrence of long-term brain damage is in dispute. Some scientists argue that Ecstasy users should be warned in the strongest possible terms about potential brain damage. Others maintain that if risks are exaggerated or go against the users' own experiences, authorities will lose credibility and their warnings will be completely ignored. The only way to find an answer to the question of whether Ecstasy causes long-term brain damage is rigorous scientific inquiry.

In a small clinic in Charleston, South Carolina, preparations are under way for a landmark medical experiment. As *New Scientist* went to press, the researchers were still waiting for final approval from an ethics panel. But if all goes to plan, a dozen or so traumatised victims of violent crime will soon be given a mind-altering substance in a bid to release them from their terrible fears.[1]

1. Final approval for MDMA experiments on human beings was not received until September 2003. The necessary Schedule I registration for researcher Michael Mithoefer was issued in March 2004.

The trial is funded by the Multidisciplinary Association for Psychedelic Studies, a maverick body founded by an enthusiast with a drugs policy PhD called Rick Doblin. And if it seems a little hippy-trippy, appearances are deceiving. Double-blinded and placebo-controlled, the trial is, on paper at least, as rigorous as anything a pharmaceuticals company might carry out. What's more, every detail has been approved by stern-faced government regulators at the US Food and Drug Administration.

> *Nobody claims ecstasy is benign. . . . Yet few . . . experts . . . believe that research has yet proved ecstasy causes lasting damage to human brain cells.*

Their colleagues over at the Drug Enforcement [Administration] are furious, and it's not hard to see why. The pill in question is [E]cstasy, otherwise known as MDMA. And in normal circumstances of course, government authorities do not see swallowing it as a remedy for the psychological effects of crime. They regard it as a crime itself, not to mention a threat to people's health. Especially in the US, where the drug's rising popularity has been rattling law enforcers.

Indeed, fearing a crack-style epidemic, the US government has in the past couple of years stiffened legal penalties and stepped up efforts to publicise the dangers. Dose for dose, ecstasy offences are now punished more harshly in the US than those involving heroin. Radio ads and posters in malls warn of memory loss. The hugely influential National Institute on Drug Abuse near Washington DC has even been distributing postcards picturing brain scans. The cards set a normal brain, looking bright and radiant, alongside a "brain after ecstasy"—a lump with dark blotches that look like holes.

Mixed messages

In other words, while bona fide doctors supported by one US government agency get ready to dole out E as a medicine, other agencies are doing their utmost to warn teenagers off the drug. It's all very confusing. And you'll find equally mixed messages elsewhere. Take Britain. Last year [2001] the government introduced a tough new law making it a crime for club owners to permit the use of ecstasy on their premises. This year it issued a booklet telling the same club owners to lay on chill-out rooms, treatment areas and plentiful supplies of water. If not a green light to ecstasy use, then surely a sign of greater tolerance . . . or maybe not. For in Britain, the law puts ecstasy on a par with heroin and crack cocaine. And while some senior British police officers think that's wrong, the government insists it will not be downgrading a substance that the evidence to date shows is so dangerous.

But just how dangerous is it? In recent years the US government has spent tens of millions of dollars, way more than anyone else, trying to pinpoint the harm. And according to its most senior scientific officials there's no longer any doubt: even if it doesn't kill you, ecstasy is a recipe for lasting, possibly permanent, damage to the serotonin neurons in the brain that are involved in everything from memory and mood to sleep, sex and appetite. In a hearing before the Senate last July [2001], NIDA's [National Institute on Drug Abuse] then director Alan Leshner stated: "There is across-the-board agreement that brain damage does occur." Research, he added, has "unequivocally shown that MDMA literally damages brain cells".

> *Some short-term problems [of ecstasy use] are no longer in serious dispute.*

New Scientist went behind the scenes to talk to a wide range of researchers. We found that no such agreement exists. Nobody claims ecstasy is benign. It isn't, and never could be—no drug is. Yet few of the experts we contacted believe that research has yet proved ecstasy causes lasting damage to human brain cells or memory. Far from it, according to some, the highest-profile evidence to date simply cannot be trusted.

Blotchy brain scans of ecstasy users have become the ace card in public information campaigns. In the US, they also strongly influenced the move to tougher sentences. Yet impartial experts told us that the scans, though published in a respected journal, are based on experiments so fundamentally flawed they risk undermining the credibility of attempts to educate people about the risks of drugs. "The brain scans do not

prove ecstasy damages serotonergic neurons," said one researcher, who asked for anonymity. "Whether to use the evidence is therefore a matter of politics rather than science."

Our enquiry doesn't prove ecstasy is harmless to brain cells. But it does raise questions key to the future of drugs policies the world over. When the evidence about the safety of an illicit drug is complex and disputed, who gets to decide which findings are sound enough to influence policy? How active should government policy makers be in screening out unreliable findings? And how open should they be about scientific dissent?

Ecstasy affects neurotransmitters

Some things about ecstasy are reasonably certain. Like many legal drugs, it affects the way brain cells handle the neurotransmitter serotonin. The cells in question are rooted near the brain's base but have long nerve fibres that fan out into higher regions. Here the fibres meet and communicate with other nerve cells, "messaging" them by squirting serotonin into the tiny joints, or synapses, that connect all nerve cells in the brain.

MDMA turns these squirts into surges. It makes cells shoot virtually their entire load of serotonin and reabsorb it unusually slowly. And the drug does this by latching onto certain proteins dotting the surfaces of the nerve cells, called serotonin transporters. The normal job of these proteins is to absorb serotonin back into cells. MDMA makes the proteins work in reverse and pump the stuff out. It's not all the drug does to brain chemistry, but most scientists think it's the key to E's [ecstasy's] loved-up sensations.

And the key, too, to the drug's less desirable effects. Some short-term problems are no longer in serious dispute. In recent years it's become clear that ecstasy can make it dangerously difficult for some people to pass water, and help to bring on sudden and sometimes fatal heatstroke, especially in hot dance clubs. Most experts also agree that by temporarily depleting the brain of serotonin, MDMA can leave users vulnerable to the mid-week blues. Yet neither of these risks, say experts, has created a serious public health problem. The mood swings are comparatively mild, and, despite the drug's massive popularity, ecstasy deaths remain extremely rare: downhill skiing kills more people. Even Britain's leading ecstasy expert, John Henry of St Mary's Hospital Medical School in London, thinks the risk of sudden death has been "overemphasised".

What most worries scientists like Henry is the possibility that hundreds of thousands of ecstasy users could be storing up mental health problems for the future. Are they? George Ricaurte and Una McCann, a husband-and-wife team at Johns Hopkins University in Baltimore, Maryland, have led the way in trying to pinpoint the drug's long-term impact on the brain. And after nearly 15 years of research, they are convinced the drug can damage serotonin synapses and nerve fibres. Indeed, they say, really persistent users even risk succumbing to "pruning", in which the longer, thicker serotonin nerve fibres in the brain wither and are replaced by a denser growth of spidery, shorter ones. In short, swallow E week in week out and the fine structure of your brain may never be the same again.

Hardly a basis for pressing for lower legal penalties. But how good is the evidence? For years it came exclusively from animal experiments. Typically, researchers give rats or monkeys high doses of ecstasy, leave them a few weeks, months or even years, and slice open their brains. It's not easy to scrutinise entire nerve fibres and synapses directly, but scientists can take a snapshot of the serotonin transporters dotted around the brain to see if any are missing or out of place. Many studies have found such changes, but some haven't, and the experiments continue to this day. So does the debate about what they really mean.

Questionable findings

In 1998, however, the case against ecstasy took a dramatic new turn. Ricaurte's team published a paper in *The Lancet* reporting what looked to be lasting brain damage in people who use ecstasy. This time the evidence was from a PET [Positron Emission Tomography] brain scanning study and seemed clear-cut. Where scans of control subjects were alive with colour, those of ecstasy users looked dull and dark. Ecstasy "injures brain for life", declared one of many startling newspaper headlines.

The study involved injecting 14 people who'd used ecstasy on average more than 100 times with chemical probes designed to stick to the serotonin transporter proteins that ecstasy targets. Wherever the probes end up they give off a detectable but safe radioactive glow. If ecstasy destroys serotonin synapses and fibres, the reasoning went, there ought to be fewer transporters for the probe to find in these damaged brains, and they ought to glow less. Sure enough, the brains of the ecstasy users did on average glow less than those of control subjects.

At the time, not every expert was convinced this deficiency was evidence of long-term damage by ecstasy. The drug users used lots of substances and the researchers reported no urine or saliva tests to prove they were drug-free at the time of the scan. Some critics even suggested the subjects could have been naturally deficient in serotonin synapses. But as it was impossible to prove these alternative explanations, the bleaker view of the brain scans took hold.

> *The evidence [that ecstasy causes brain damage] is not . . . clear-cut.*

Soon the scans were at the centre of the US government's campaign on the dangers of club drugs and featuring in TV documentaries. The scans also featured prominently in the official report by the US Sentencing Commission that last year led to longer prison sentences for ecstasy offences. The brains scans, it claimed, showed "that users had a significantly reduced number of serotonin transporters throughout the brain".

And soon too other brain-imaging teams were attempting to build on the 1998 finding. A year later, researchers from the Royal Edinburgh Hospital in Scotland also published a paper claiming that regular ecstasy users have fewer serotonin transporters in the brain—further evidence, they concluded, of the drug's "neurotoxicity".

Women are more susceptible than men

More recently, a team led by Liesbeth Reneman and Gerard den Heeten of the Academic Medical Centre in Amsterdam wanted to find out if heavier users of ecstasy lose more serotonin synapses than lighter users. To this end, they scanned the brains of four groups: moderate users of ecstasy who claimed to have taken no more than 50 tablets in their lifetime; heavy users who claimed to have taken hundreds; heavy users who claimed to have abstained for at least a year; and a control group. "Our results," the team concluded in a paper published last year in *The Lancet*, "indicate that women could be more susceptible than men to the neurotoxic effects of MDMA".

It was another worrying finding that on the face of it seemed to back up the crucial 1998 study. Except that on close inspection, there were discrepancies and contradictions. This time, the male ecstasy brains in the study lit up just as much as the control brains, and it was only after analysing the female brains separately from the male brains that the researchers found anything different about some of the women. The brains of the heavy female users, it turned out, did light up less than those of the moderate female users and female controls. Yet even these "damaged" female brains performed no worse than the brains of the supposedly healthy male non-users.

It's a confusing picture, so *New Scientist* asked some leading independent scientists to look at the evidence afresh. What we learned was that the probes used in the scanning studies have serious deficiencies and that despite the poster depiction of "your brain on ecstasy", there never was—and never has been—a typical scan showing the typical brain of a long-term ecstasy user.

"There are no holes in the brains of ecstasy users," says Stephen Kish, a neuropathologist at the Center for Addiction and Health in Toronto. "And if anyone wants a straightforward answer to whether ecstasy causes any brain damage, it's impossible to get one from these papers." Marc Laruelle, a Columbia University expert on brain scanning probes, agrees: "All the papers have very significant scientific limitations that make me uneasy."

Imprecise measurements

According to both experts, the key flaw in the 1998 study is the sheer variability of the measurements. Some control brains performed up to 40 times better than others, and even some of the ecstasy brains outshone control brains by factors of 10 or more—a level of scatter that both experts say is unprecedented in this type of study. According to Kish, the huge variations seen even in the healthy controls are a sure sign that the probe failed to give precise and reliable measurements. It's taken years for the problem to surface, says Kish, because the full range of the scatter is obscured in the original paper by the unusual way the researchers analysed their findings, converting the raw brain scan measurements into logarithms before plotting them out.

So why the unreliability? Laruelle says the probes used in all the ecstasy brain scan studies don't always stick just to serotonin transporters and should therefore only be used in certain brain areas. In recent years, his team has established that only the midbrain, thalamus and striatum have enough serotonin transporters to give reliable readings. None of the ecstasy studies focused exclusively on these structures. The Edinburgh team looked only at the cerebral cortex.

> *If there are any suspicions at all [that ecstasy causes cognitive impairment], governments and scientists should make the strongest possible statements about risk.*

Ricaurte rejects the criticism. "Variability in the data would lessen our ability to detect differences between groups and, potentially, lead to an underestimation of differences between MDMA users and controls," he told *New Scientist.* "The fact that significant differences were found speaks for itself."

When it comes down to it, what brains look like in a scanner shouldn't matter as much as whether ecstasy has any noticeable long-term effect on the way people think, feel and act. So does it? There's certainly been a rash of papers in psychology journals suggesting ecstasy users have poorer memories and mental reflexes than nonusers. And some of the conclusions make disturbing reading. In one typical study, ecstasy users "showed significantly poorer verbal fluency and immediate and delayed recall". In another, they were "worse on a sustained attention task requiring arithmetic calculations, a task requiring short-term memory and a task of semantic recognition and verbal reasoning". Last year one British team even equated such symptoms with those seen early on in Alzheimer's disease.

Yet take a closer look and, as with the brain scans, the evidence is not as clear-cut as it sounds. For a start, in the majority of tests of mental agility, ecstasy users perform just as well as non-users. Their reaction times, visual memories and ability to concentrate all come out looking normal—sometimes better than normal.

Test results are confusing

In one study, psychologist Andrew Parrott of the University of East London and his team found ecstasy users outperforming non-users in tests requiring them to rotate complex shapes in their mind's eye. Ecstasy users also had the edge on non-users when it came to searching a series of virtual rooms on a computer screen to find a small red toy car. Afterwards, says Parrott, the ecstasy users were better at answering questions about the shapes of the rooms and the positions of their doors.

Where ecstasy users do seem to perform worse is in learning new verbal information. In tests where people are given lists of words and then asked to recall them later, a group of non-users might score an average of, say, 10 out of 15, while a group of ecstasy users of the same age and social background might get 8. According to Parrott, who published the first finding of this type in 1998, ecstasy users are also slower on average to improve when the test is repeated. But their performance still lies well within the spectrum of what counts as normal.

> *Nobody can yet put their hands on their heart and say that none of them [recreational users of ecstasy] will ever have serious mental health problems.*

In other words, whatever ecstasy's cognitive effects may be, they are subtle. So subtle that some experts think it's jumping the gun to blame ecstasy when most users of the drug take many other substances. A team at Imperial College Medical School in London recently tested three different groups for recall, word fluency and speed of thought. One used no drugs, another just cannabis, and the third both ecstasy and cannabis. On average, the "no drugs" group performed the best. But the "just cannabis" people scored no better than those who used ecstasy and cannabis. So is cannabis—a drug people often smoke to "come down" from an ecstasy high—the real problem?

Or are scientists worrying about a cognitive impairment that just isn't there? It's an open secret that some teams have failed to find deficits in ecstasy users and had trouble publishing the findings. "The journals are very conservative," says Parrott. "It's a source of bias." Parrott himself has had two papers of this sort turned down.

But is any of this a reason to dilute the ecstasy health warnings? Surely if there are any suspicions at all, governments and scientists should make the strongest possible statements about risk. Perhaps. But some in the field feel this approach carries a risk of its own. If people think the health warnings are exaggerated or at odds with their own experience of the drug, the authorities risk losing credibility, and with it their chance to educate anyone about drugs.

Kish says many of the ecstasy users he interacts with already consider the brain scans to be "simply unbelievable". Harry Sumnall, who studies ecstasy users at the University of Liverpool, fears that by prematurely highlighting the drug as especially dangerous, psychologists and the media risk giving out the false message that "as long as you stay away from E, you'll be fine".

Double standards

The situation isn't helped by the impression that double standards are at work, with one set of rules for prescription drugs and much stricter rules for drugs used illicitly. While scores of studies have looked for evidence of biochemical changes in the brains of animals and people exposed to ecstasy, only a handful have looked for anything similar in brains exposed to antidepressants and other prescribed agents that act on the serotonin transporter. And when scientists do scrutinise such drugs, officials don't jump so readily to alarming conclusions.

In the 1980s, for instance, Ricaurte's team began publishing papers suggesting a diet pill, taken daily by millions, called fenfluramine could damage brain cells. The evidence was strikingly similar to that seen in animals given ecstasy. But while ecstasy's "neurotoxicity" triggered government action, fenfluramine's was brushed aside.

Of course, many people feel more comfortable about prescribed medicines carrying risks, because they provide benefits too. That's why Rick Doblin's efforts to turn MDMA into a prescription pill could be so crucial to reversing the drug's demonisation. Anecdotal evidence already suggests ecstasy could ease the pain and fears of patients with cancer or post-traumatic stress disorder, and perhaps even help Parkinson's sufferers. But Doblin knows only evidence from the most rigorous of rigorous trials will do. There's no evidence, he says, that the low doses the patients will be getting could damage serotonin nerve fibres. Yet nor will the pills be instant miracle cures: each patient in the Charleston trial will have 16 hours of psychiatric counselling as well.

And the hundreds of thousands of recreational users? Nobody can yet put their hands on their heart and say that none of them will ever have serious mental health problems, especially the heavy users, but this drug is not new, says Doblin. "I first tried it in 1982, and many of the early users are now in their 50s and 60s. We are not flooding into treatment centres."

5

Club Drugs Facilitate Rape

Nora Fitzgerald and K. Jack Riley

Nora Fitzgerald is a social science analyst at the National Institute of Justice. K. Jack Riley is director of the Criminal Justice Program at RAND, a nonprofit organization that provides analysis of complicated problems in the public and private sectors.

Two common club drugs, Rohypnol and GHB (gamma-hydroxybutyrate), are being used to facilitate rape by immobilizing victims and impairing their memories. Because Rohypnol and GHB are often mixed into victims' drinks without their knowledge, victims may not immediately realize that they have been assaulted, which delays their visit to the police or rape counselor, making it difficult to obtain evidence of rape and gauge the prevalence of the problem. Increased club drug interdiction and community awareness programs have been initiated to help curb the problem of drug-facilitated rape.

More than 430,000 sexual assaults occur annually in the United States, according to victimization surveys. Many of these assaults involve alcohol and drugs, which are often used voluntarily by both victim and offender. But in the mid and late 1990's, ethnographers and rape crisis centers began hearing reports of drugs, often referred to as "roofies" and "liquid ecstasy," being administered clandestinely to immobilize victims, impair their memory, and thus facilitate rape. Two drugs in particular were mentioned in these reports: Rohypnol (the pharmaceutical trade name for flunitrazepam) and GHB (gamma-hydroxybutyrate).

Nora Fitzgerald and K. Jack Riley, "Drug-Facilitated Rape: Looking for the Missing Pieces," *National Institute of Justice Journal*, April 2000.

These drugs can produce loss of consciousness and the inability to recall recent events. Victims may not be aware that they have ingested drugs or that they have been raped while under the influence of drugs. Reports of such assaults and increases in the recreational consumption of the drugs used in these assaults have brought drug-facilitated rape into sharp focus in recent years.

This article summarizes findings about drug-facilitated rape learned by researchers at the U.S. Department of Justice in response to a request from the Attorney General for more information about this new phenomenon.

Rape-facilitating drugs

Sexual assault victims who believe drugs were surreptitiously given to them typically report remembering sensations of drunkenness that do not correspond with the amounts of alcohol consumed, unexplained gaps in memory, altered levels of consciousness, and unexplainable signs of physical trauma. The most commonly implicated drugs are Rohypnol and GHB.

Rohypnol, or flunitrazepam, belongs to a class of drugs called benzodiazepines and is approved for use in 80 countries, but not in the United States or Canada. It is available only in pill form, is tasteless, odorless, and colorless, and dissolves to some degree in liquid.

Benzodiazepines are used primarily to produce sedation, sleep, or muscle relaxation; to reduce seizures and anxiety; and to produce anterograde amnesia, a desired effect for some surgical procedures. *Anterograde* amnesia is a condition in which events that occurred during the time the drug was in effect are forgotten, in contrast to *retrograde* amnesia, in which events prior to the intervening agent are forgotten.

Rohypnol mentally and physically incapacitates an individual, particularly when used in combination with alcohol, and is capable of producing anterograde amnesia.

GHB, a drug first synthesized in the 1920's, occurs naturally in the human body in minute amounts. It was under development as an anesthetic agent in the late 1950's and early 1960's, but no commercial products were developed from these efforts. Until the FDA [Food and Drug Administration] banned the drug in 1990, it was available through health food stores and marketed as both a sleep aid and as a body-building supplement. Several vendors distributed products containing GHB under trade names such as "Gamma Hydrate" and "Somatomax PM."

GHB is marketed in some European countries as an adjunct to anesthesia and currently is being tested for treatment of narcolepsy as well as alcohol addiction and withdrawal (with mixed results) in Europe and the United States.

The prevalence of use

No one really knows how common drug-facilitated rape is because today's research tools do not offer a means of measuring the number of incidents. However, recent findings from ethnographic research and school-based surveys can provide insight into the voluntary use of these drugs.

Flunitrazepam first appeared in early warning ethonographic systems in December 1993, when it was reported among Miami high school students.

By 1995, the Community Epidemiology Working Group (CEWG) found that use of Rohypnol was spreading in Florida and Texas. Pulse Check [an ethnographic reporting system] reported Rohypnol use was rising, particularly among youth and young adults. Ethnographers in Florida and Texas reported that local law enforcement agents were seizing more Rohypnol tablets, often still in the manufacturer's packaging.

> *//* *Victims may not be aware that they have ingested drugs or . . . been raped while under the influence of drugs. //*

In 1996, Monitoring the Future (MTF) [an ongoing survey of 8th, 10th, and 12th grade students] began tracking Rohypnol. In 1999, MTF found that 0.5 percent of 8th graders and 1.0 percent of 10th and 12th graders had reported using Rohypnol in 1998, a level slightly below those found a year earlier. Such rates appear low in comparison to marijuana or amphetamine use, but they are not trivial—10th and 12th graders report similar levels of heroin use.

In 1997, Pulse Check noted that although Rohypnol continued to be available in Florida and Texas, distribution had slowed.

In 1998, Texas' statewide student survey, which uses the same methodology and many of the same items as MTF, found that 1.3 to 2.1 percent of Texas students in grades 8 to 12 reported use of Rohypnol during the school year. Later in 1998, Pulse Check reported that Rohypnol was in use in Florida, Hawaii, Minnesota, and Texas.

Mention of widespread recreational use of GHB only recently has been reported by CEWG in December 1997. In winter 1998, Pulse Check reported use of GHB in many urban areas.

The Drug Abuse Warning Network (DAWN) [which records instances of emergency room visits and deaths related to particular drugs] also has captured information about GHB because of overdoses. The Drug Enforcement Administration has documented approximately 650 overdoses and 20 deaths related to GHB. MTF added questions about GHB to its year 2000 survey.

Available law enforcement statistics on seizures and trafficking (primarily from the Drug Enforcement Administration) tend to corroborate the ethnographic and survey data.

Ethnographic measures may not represent the true scale of the drugs' use, however, and more rigorous scientific measures have not been in place long enough to give researchers the ability to project accurate trends.

> *Although . . . measuring methods do not reveal . . . how widespread drug-facilitated rape is, research does make it clear that the risk is real.*

Another factor complicating science's ability to measure the incidence and prevalence of these drugs is the lack of law enforcement evidence. Investigations of suspected drug-facilitated assaults often turn out to be inconclusive because many victims do not seek assistance until hours or days later, in part because the drugs have impaired recall and in part because victims may not recognize the signs of sexual assault. By the time they do report a suspected assault, conclusive forensic evidence may have been lost. Even when victims do suspect a drug-facilitated rape and seek help immediately, law enforcement agencies may not know how to collect evidence appropriately or how to test urine using the sensitive method required. . . .

To add more complexity to the puzzle, school-based surveys seem to suggest that Rohypnol and GHB are consumed voluntarily, perhaps increasingly so, because these drugs are cheap, easy to share, and easy to hide. Use appears to be concentrated among populations that also are at the highest risk of sexual assault, including middle school, high school, and college-age students.

The good news is that public awareness about the drugs and their effects appears to be increasing.

Real risk

Although current measuring methods do not reveal exactly how widespread drug-facilitated rape is, research does make it clear that the risk is real.

Since reports of drug-facilitated rape first started appearing, policy-makers at the Federal level have moved to address the situation. One step was to improve enforcement at the U.S.-Mexican border of the ban on importation of flunitrazepam. Then in October 1996, President [Bill] Clinton signed the Drug-Induced Rape Prevention and Punishment Act, which provides harsh penalties for distribution or possession of flunitrazepam. In February 2000, the President signed similar legislation related to GHB.

The Office for Victims of Crime (OVC) within the Department of Justice currently is providing training and technical assistance for a model program designed to promote promising practices in sexual assault medical evidentiary exams. The program, which promotes the use of specially trained sexual assault nurse examiners, has developed a guide that addresses the issues of drug-facilitated rape, with specific information and guidance regarding comprehensive drug testing and an exam protocol.

National and local victim service organizations have responded to the situation by developing campaigns to raise awareness. A Los Angeles County task force developed a rape kit and procedures designed to improve the way evidence is gathered in suspected cases of drug-facilitated rape. The task force members included the Rape Treatment Center at Santa Monica—UCLA Medical Center, the Los Angeles County District Attorney's Office, the Los Angeles Police Department, and the County of Los Angeles Sheriff's Department crime labs. . . .

Where to go from here

To understand more about drug-facilitated rape, a research agenda should include the following:

- Expansion of existing Federal data systems to provide information on drug-facilitated rape. *The National Crime Victimization Survey* may be an appropriate means for collecting population-based information on the incidence of this offense.
- Collection of new data in the fields of pharmacology and offender profiling.
- Ethnographic studies to develop a better understanding of the nature of this offense, including the most likely victims and the risk factors for victimization.
- A major multiyear, multimethod research initiative structured as four separate studies designed to measure the incidence of drug-facilitated rape among suspected cases, within the general population, among high-risk populations, and in the context of acquaintance rape.
- Funding for development of new drug detection technologies, such as hair analysis methods.

Some of the ethnographic and newspaper reporting on Rohypnol and GHB, which the Department of Justice working group tracked, has been driven in part by sporadic signs of increased recreational use and overdoses. But the more important impetus for further study appears to be reports from people who turn to rape counseling centers and clinics with complaints and suspicions that they have been victimized.

6

Ecstasy Helps Heal the Trauma of Rape

Lisa

Lisa wrote this viewpoint detailing how MDMA (Ecstasy) helped her deal with being raped and published it on the Multidisciplinary Association for Psychedelic Studies' Web site.

Lisa recounts her experience with Ecstasy and explains how, after years of conventional psychotherapy, it was Ecstasy that finally helped her heal from the trauma of rape. Ecstasy empowered Lisa and enabled her to truly connect with others for the first time since her assault. She urges the federal government to allow researchers to explore the therapeutic effects of this drug.

MDMA can soothe the pain and terror that still gnaws at a person's core years . . . even decades . . . after sexual assault. One dose in the right setting improved the rest of my life in profound and subtle ways. I don't sit with my arms and legs folded tightly as a signal to stay away nearly as much as I used to. I am in love with a man I trust. And my nightmares have finally changed.

For over 20 years, the dream scenario was almost always the same. I would frantically struggle with numb fingers to lock multiple locks on one side of a door as my attacker on the other side was unlocking them with superhuman speed. Since I took MDMA with the intention of receiving its therapeutic benefit, I no longer wake up feebly gasping the word, "help," aloud even though it feels as if I'm screaming my brains out with no hope of anyone arriving in time to save me.

Although I had good results with conventional therapy and

a short-course of prescription antidepressants, part of me was not fully restored. I'd read accounts of how LSD had been used in therapy before it became illegal, and I'd wondered at times if it might unlock the cogs in my soul that were jammed. The potential of hallucinating—without a firm grasp on reality—that I was again in the presence of the babysitter who molested me when I was seven or the guy who raped me when I was 18 was too threatening. I just knew I was a bad acid trip waiting to happen, so I turned down a few opportunities to try it when I was younger.

Taking MDMA, commonly known as Ecstasy, was my way of securing the help that didn't arrive when I was little or over-powered. And it worked. For me, Ecstasy was sanctuary—a few hours in the safest place I'd ever been.

> *Ecstasy was sanctuary—a few hours in the safest place I'd ever been.*

I had heard a few anecdotal accounts from acquaintances about what the experience was like for them. Like most people probably do at first, I assumed it was a feel-good party drug—a less sinister cousin to cocaine. Something too risky and illegal for me to even consider. I was well into my professional life with a divorce behind me before I learned that dozens of therapists used MDMA successfully as a supplement to therapy in the 70's and 80's for a wide range of clinical applications.

So, at the age of 36, after not even being in the same room with any drugs since college, I set out to self-treat myself in the best situation available at the time.

A warehouse rave

I wanted so badly to turn the whole evening into an "all about me" therapy session. I had fantasies about the kind of experience I've since heard referred to as the "sacramental use of empathic substances." Something very new-agey and ritualistic. But considering that others in the group had never tried it before and those who had didn't want to spend the evening getting in touch with my feelings (even though they're all very decent people and supportive friends), I decided it would be far too selfish and actually rude to demand special attention.

As unique as the evening seemed at the time, this next part will sound like a bit of a cliché. We took a cab to an underground club. It was my first and only rave. It wasn't a huge gathering in the desert or in a derelict warehouse. It was just a big basement downtown packed with kids and an enormous sound system. I had only agreed to go after we made a plan to leave early enough to spend time just talking and listening to music back at home.

> *With MDMA, the conquest mentality gets replaced with a desire to connect on a much more friendly and dignified level.*

I knew I'd be half a generation older than most of the other people at the club. So, I wasted a ridiculous amount of time worrying about things like whether or not I'd stick out because I was wearing the wrong shoes. A friend who knew this scene assured me that no one there could care less about my footwear. I had no idea how right she was.

I was starting to feel really out of place and somewhat threatened when we descended the first set of stairs to a table where a young girl and a bouncer-type were selling tickets. It was the familiar feeling of losing access to all the exits—of being profoundly trapped. I paid my fifteen bucks, and as she reached out to stamp my hand, the girl gazed up at me and airily sighed, "She's beautiful." Her comment was so welcoming. Of course, I suspected it was drug inspired, but nevertheless my self-consciousness began to diminish from that point on. I had a comforting feeling that the people here wouldn't judge me harshly.

After watching the dance floor for a few minutes, we noticed about seven people huddled together in a conspicuous group hug. I turned to my friends and said smugly, "No way in hell that's going to be us." Little did I know.

Casting off fear

I noticed that an organization dedicated to promoting safety in clubs was on duty here making sure water, cooled rooms, and educational literature was available. Feeling reasonably well-protected by my friends, I went ahead and swallowed one pill from a batch that checked out as okay on an Internet rating site and had passed a chemical screening test. And then I waited. . . .

I'm not going to try to describe the sensations of the high. There are lots of other sources for first-hand accounts of what MDMA feels like—especially on the Internet. Some accounts focus on the physical experience while others try to convey the emotional or spiritual significance they discover.

Beyond the high, there are three ways in which the drug helped me cast off some of the lingering trauma I'd been suffering for years.

The first new awareness that came to me was social. I noticed a stark contrast between this club scene and the one I knew from my youth. When I went out dancing in high school and college, everyone dressed to impress . . . usually all in black. We wore pouty scowls, acted coolly indifferent, and danced with self-conscious awareness about whether or not we were "doing it right." And there was an ever-present "meat market" vibe.

With MDMA, the conquest mentality gets replaced with a desire to connect on a much more friendly and dignified level. It was indescribably healing to be in a male-dominated crowd and never once have the sensation that I was being ogled, stalked, chatted up, or hit on. And it wasn't because of my age, either. The male attention I received was gentle and appreciative. Periodically, I'd be treated to a fantastical light show when a young man with glow sticks would politely approach me and wait for an indication that I would enjoy such a treat. After about one-minute of watching whizzing, glowing lights all around my field of vision with rapture, we'd exchange an appreciative smile, and then he'd move on to share the great sensation.

> *It [Ecstasy] can create a safe way to confront deep fears with a lasting benefit that extends beyond the high.*

I believe that only a percentage . . . probably not even the majority of people at the club that night were on MDMA. But I think that enough of them have experienced its effects in a meaningful way that propagate a lasting respect for others who are there to enjoy the music, the vibe, and each other . . . regardless of gender. I've read about theories that suggest that soccer hooliganism in Britain declined rapidly with the introduction of MDMA into the scene in England. For the same reasons that sworn enemies from rival soccer clubs became peaceful ravers together, I think the prevalence of male violence against women could diminish—at least in the short term—as an effect of experiencing the self-love and empathy MDMA can provide.

Rational thought is not impaired

For this reason, I was greatly saddened when I did a Web search using the words "MDMA" and "Rape" and found only two articles related to the therapeutic benefits for rape victims. All the others either directly or indirectly lumped MDMA into the Date Rape Drug category, giving what I believe is a false impression that sexual predators use it to subdue victims. I haven't come across any studies that take a serious look at whether MDMA contributes to increased violence against women or if this drug can actually help diminish it.

The best sensation was feeling no fear.

My second point underscores the validity of the view that MDMA does not impair rational thought. It is not a hallucinogenic drug. And further, it can create a safe way to confront deep fears with a lasting benefit that extends beyond the high. And here's how I know:

The other woman in our group had done Ecstasy before, so she was an effective guide who could gently enhance the experience for those of us who were new to it. At the beginning of the peak, she simply ran the tips of her fingers down the front of my forearm as an entirely non-erotic invitation to come out and play. It was her clever way of saying, "See what intense pleasure you're capable of feeling now?" After being locked away in my head, after floating somewhat disembodied without the sensation of feeling my feet on the ground, without ever really feeling sexy due to sexual assault, I was suddenly free.

I started to dance like a belly-dancer and a goddess, like a teenager and whole mature woman all at once. I had been dancing with my eyes closed, with pleasure and enough abandon to draw attention when I suddenly felt a hand on my shoulder and stopped. I opened my eyes to see a man's face inches from mine, and he was shouting at me to be heard above the loud music. He could have been the stranger in my nightmares.

He had thick furrowed eyebrows, squinty eyes, and a hard set to his jaw. He held one arm behind his back. "Does he have a weapon back there?" I thought. "Is he poised to flash his badge and haul me off to jail?" He continued shouting until I could hear him say, "What are you on?" It's very hard to lie under the influence of MDMA, and I've always been too polite for my own good, so I replied, "No, thank you." Again, he yelled, "What are you on? E? Acid? Alcohol?" I was afraid of being arrested, so again, I said, "No. Thank you." Finally, he revealed that he was holding water behind his back, and then I understood that he was probably a volunteer or someone affiliated with the club trying to prevent dehydration. But could I trust that his bottle wasn't spiked with something dangerous? Knowing I could get water from my friends, I said, "No. Thank you. I'm fine," just as my friend approached.

Another chance for help

She'd been accosted by him too and got the same creepy feeling I did. She comforted me and led me back to the rest of our group. This was the hallucination I had feared when I considered taking LSD, only this was real. I was alone in a situation that should have horrified me, but I stayed calm and when I returned to my group of friends, something very unexpected happened as a result of this encounter. By suddenly being put back into a threatening situation with overtones of the abuse I'd suffered in my youth, I got another chance to ask for healing, loving help. I felt vulnerable, but my rational mind was guiding me the entire time.

The third benefit was a sort of temporal cocoon that let me determine the personal gain I'd receive from this form of self-therapy. MDMA gave me a second opportunity to metamorphosize. When I got back to the group, we were all experiencing intense sensations, including the common urge to babble. I wanted everybody to stop, be still, and hug me. And I wanted to hug them too and express kind thoughts. I wanted them to listen to me and speak to me in soothing voices. But everyone had impressions and observations to share, and I didn't want to cause a scene. It felt somewhat similar to not being able to yell out in my nightmares, but without any fear present.

It was so loud in the club that we ended up breaking up in little groups of two or three. Even though we drew our faces near to each other in order to be heard over the music, we still had to shout a little. I gradually became aware that I was using a voice that was familiar and yet unlike my natural speaking voice. It was the voice of a little girl. The 7-year-old me had showed up unexpectedly. The little girl's voice just came out without intention on my part. She was going to speak even if I wasn't. My friends didn't know it, but they were babysitting me for a while there.

> *The argument that it [Ecstasy] has no medical purpose is a falsehood.*

For a couple of hours, I had a strong sensation of being little again. I was curious, sweet, precocious, and imaginative. It felt good to be in my body, and I assumed a child's posture and gestures. I wasn't self-conscious at all. I wasn't sexual, but I recovered an ability to be extremely intimate and express just what I was thinking. I was excited and impulsive and confident. I was open to making new friends just because they were people I liked . . . just like when I was seven. But the best sensation was feeling no fear.

The affects of the MDMA wore off slowly and gently, and it had a lingering pleasant effect all weekend. But beyond that, my nightmares stopped and then changed. I had the first one a couple of weeks ago. This time, instead of cowering and screaming behind the unlocking door, I grabbed a tool . . . a hammer . . . to fight back. I woke up before I attacked my attacker, but with the sensation that I would bash his head in if I had too.

Ecstasy research should be encouraged

Why did I have to break the law to receive this healing? Why did I have to take such risks? My preference would have been to be with my therapist in a safe setting with loved ones who were committed to promoting healing. I would want a medical doctor present if rare complications presented. I would want to know with the greatest degree of certainty that I was taking the dose appropriate for my physiology. I would want to extend the benefit by having follow-up sessions with my therapist to maximize the therapeutic effect.

I've learned a lot since I made the hard decision to break the law in order to heal myself, but I still don't understand why there's been no responsible, FDA [Food and Drug Administration]-approved clinical testing of MDMA in this country since 1985. The argument that it has no medical purpose is a falsehood. It simply isn't true. We haven't taken the steps we need to in order to secure its tremendous social and personal humanitarian and pharmacological benefits.

We can't know what relief or rehabilitation this drug could offer to schizophrenics, psychotics, rape victims, addicts, gang members, those in chronic pain from disease, grief, or other trauma if scientists and research institutions can not complete credible, unbiased investigations.

We will all find more meaning in our lives when we are finally brave enough to push beyond our timidity and ignorance . . . when we choose caring for one another as our highest priority.

7

The Sexual Effects of Ecstasy Are Exaggerated

Jacob Sullum

Jacob Sullum is senior editor of Reason *magazine.*

While MDMA (Ecstasy) is popularly associated with increased sexual desire, its true effect is emotional and sensual, not sexual. In fact, most people find it difficult to perform sexually after ingesting Ecstasy. Thus, parental fears about the sexual effects of Ecstasy on young people are misguided. Labeling Ecstasy an aphrodesiac is simply part of a long-standing tradition in the United States of linking wanton sexual acts with the latest drug popular among youth.

[I]n the] spring [of 2001], the Chicago City Council decided "to crack down on wild rave parties that lure youngsters into environments loaded with dangerous club drugs, underage drinking and sometimes predatory sexual behavior," as the *Chicago Tribune* put it. The newspaper described raves as "one-night-only parties . . . often held in warehouses or secret locations where people pay to dance, do drugs, play loud music, and engage in random sex acts." Taking a dim view of such goings-on, the city council passed an ordinance threatening to jail building owners or managers who allowed raves to be held on their property. Mayor Richard Daley took the occasion to "lash out at the people who produce the huge rogue dance parties where Ecstasy and other designer drugs are widely used." In Daley's view, rave promoters were deliberately seducing the innocent. "They are after all of our children," he warned. "Par-

Jacob Sullum, "Sex, Drugs, and Techno Music: Why the Rap Against Ecstasy Has a Familiar Ring to It," *Reason*, vol. 33, January 2000. Copyright © 2000 by the Reason Foundation, 3415 S. Sepulveda Blvd., Suite 400, Los Angeles, CA 90034, www.reason.com. Reproduced by permission.

ents should be outraged by this."

The reaction against raves reflects familiar anxieties about what the kids are up to, especially when it comes to sex. As the chemical symbol of raves, MDMA—a.k.a. Ecstasy—has come to represent sexual abandon and, partly through association with other "club drugs," sexual assault. These are not the only fears raised by MDMA. The drug, whose full name is methylenedioxymethamphetamine, has also been accused of causing brain damage and of leading people astray with ersatz feelings of empathy and euphoria (concerns discussed later in this [viewpoint]). But the sexual angle is interesting because it has little to do with the drug's actual properties, a situation for which there is considerable precedent in the history of reputed aphrodisiacs.

A relative of both amphetamine and mescaline, MDMA is often described as a stimulant with psychedelic qualities. But its effects are primarily emotional, without the perceptual changes caused by LSD. Although MDMA was first synthesized by the German drug company Merck in 1912, it did not gain a following until the 1970s, when the psychonautical chemist Alexander Shulgin, a Dow researcher turned independent consultant, tried some at the suggestion of a graduate student he was helping a friend supervise. "It was not a psychedelic in the visual or interpretive sense," he later wrote, "but the lightness and warmth of the psychedelic was present and quite remarkable." MDMA created a "window," he decided. "It enabled me to see out, and to see my own insides, without distortions or reservations."

> *The sexual angle is interesting because it has little to do with the drug's actual properties.*

After observing some striking examples of people who claimed to have overcome serious personal problems (including a severe stutter and oppressive guilt) with the help of MDMA, Shulgin introduced the drug to a psychologist he knew who had already used psychedelics as an aid to therapy. "Adam," the pseudonym that Shulgin gave him (also a nickname for the drug), was on the verge of retiring, but was so impressed by MDMA's effects that he decided to continue working. He shared his techniques with other psychologists and psychiatrists, and under his influence thousands of people reportedly used the drug to enhance communication and self-insight. "It seemed to dissolve fear for a few hours," says a psychiatrist who tried MDMA in the early '80s. "I thought it would have been very useful for working with people with trauma disorders." Shulgin concedes that the was "a hint of snake-oil" in MDMA's reputed versatility, but he himself considered it "an incredible tool." He quotes one psychiatrist as saying, "MDMA is penicillin for the soul, and you don't give up penicillin, once you've seen what it can do."

Banned in 1985

Shulgin did not see MDMA exclusively as a psychotherapeutic tool. He also referred to it as "my low-calorie martini," a way of loosening up and relating more easily to others at social gatherings. This aspect of the drug came to the fore in the '80s, when MDMA became popular among nightclubbers in Texas, where it was marketed as a party drug under the name Ecstasy. The open recreational use of Ecstasy at clubs in Dallas and Austin brought down the wrath of the Drug Enforcement Administration, which decided to put MDMA in the same legal category as heroin. Researchers who emphasized the drug's psychotherapeutic potential opposed the ban. "We had no idea psychiatrists were using it," a DEA [Drug Enforcement Administration], pharmacologist told *Newsweek* in 1985. Nor did they care: Despite an administrative law judge's recommendation that doctors be allowed to prescribe the drug, the ban on MDMA took effect the following year.

Thus MDMA followed the same pattern as LSD, moving from discreet psychotherapeutic use to the sort of conspicuous consumption that was bound to provoke a government reaction. Like LSD, it became illegal because too many people started to enjoy it. Although the DEA probably would have sought to ban any newly popular intoxicant, the name change certainly didn't help. In *Ecstasy: The MDMA Story*, Bruce Eisner quotes a distributor who claimed to have originated the name Ecstasy. He said he picked it "because it would sell better than calling it 'Empathy.' 'Empathy' would be more appropriate, but how many people know what it means?" In its traditional sense, ecstasy has a spiritual connotation, but in common usage it simply means intense pleasure—often the kind associated with sex. As David Smith, director of the Haight-Ashbury Free Clinic, observed, the name "suggested that it made sex better." Some marketers have been more explicit: A 1999 article in the *Journal of Toxicology* (headlined "SEX on the Streets of Cincinnati") reported an analysis of "unknown tablets imprinted with 'SEX'" that turned out to contain MDMA.

Hyperbolic comments by some users have reinforced Ecstasy's sexual connotations. "One enthusiast described the feeling as a six-hour orgasm!" exclaimed the author of a 2000 op-ed piece in Malaysia's *New Straits Times*, picking up a phrase quoted in *Time* a couple of months before. A column in *The Toronto Sun*, meanwhile, stated matter-of-factly that MDMA "can even make you feel like a six-hour orgasm." If simply taking MDMA makes you feel that way, readers might reasonably conclude, MDMA-enhanced sex must be indescribably good.

> **" *Like LSD, [Ecstasy] became illegal because too many people started to enjoy it.* "**

Another reason MDMA came to be associated with sex is its reputation as a "hug drug" that breaks down emotional barriers and brings out feelings of affection. The warmth and candor of people who've taken MDMA may be interpreted as flirtatiousness. More generally, MDMA is said to remove fear, which is one reason psychotherapists have found it so useful. The same effect could also be described as a loss of inhibitions, often a precursor to sexual liaisons. Finally, users report enhanced pleasure from physical sensations, especially the sense of touch. They often trade hugs, caresses, and back rubs.

MDMA and sex do not go well together

Yet the consensus among users seems to be that MDMA's effects are more sensual than sexual. According to a therapist quoted by Jerome Beck and Marsha Rosenbaum in their book *Pursuit of Ecstasy*, "MDMA and sex do not go very well together. For most people, MDMA turns off the ability to function as a lover, to put it indelicately. It's called the love drug because it opens up the capacity to feel loving and affectionate and trusting." At the same time, however, it makes the "focusing of the body and the psychic energy necessary to achieve orgasm . . . very difficult. And most men find it impossible. . . . So it is a love drug but not a sex drug for most people."

Although this distinction is widely reported by users, press coverage has tended to perpetuate the connection between MDMA and sex. In 1985 *Newsweek* said the drug "is considered an aphrodisiac," while *Maclean's* played up one user's claim of "very good sexual possibilities." *Life* also cited "the drug's reputation for good sex," even while noting that it "blocks male ejaculation." More recently, a 2000 story about MDMA in *Time* began by describing "a classic Southeast Asian den of iniquity" where prostitutes used Ecstasy so they could be "friendly and outgoing." It warned that "because users feel empathetic, ecstasy can lower sexual inhibitions. Men generally cannot get erections when high on e[ecstasy], but they are often ferociously randy when its effects begin to fade." The story cited a correlation between MDMA use and "unprotected sex." A cautionary article in *Cosmopolitan* began with the account of "a 28-year-old lawyer from Los Angeles" who brought home a man with whom she felt "deeply connected" under the influence of MDMA. "We would have had sex, but he couldn't get an erection," she reported. "The next day, I was horrified that I had let a guy I couldn't even stand into my bed!"

> *[The word] ecstasy has a spiritual connotation . . . in common usage it . . . means intense pleasure—often the kind associated with sex.*

MDMA has been linked not just to regrettable sexual encounters but to rapes in which drugs are used as weapons. The connection is usually made indirectly, by way of other drugs whose effects are quite different but which are also popular at raves and dance clubs. In particular, the depressants GHB and Rohypnol have acquired reputations as "date rape drugs," used to incapacitate victims to whom they are given surreptitiously. Needless to say, this is not the main use for these substances, which people generally take on purpose because they like their effects. It's not clear exactly how often rapists use GHB or Rohypnol, but such cases are surely much rarer than the hysterical reaction from the press and Congress (which passed a Date Rape Drug Prohibition Act last year [2001]) would lead one to believe. The public has nonetheless come to view these intoxicants primarily as instruments of assault, an impression that has affected the image of other "club drugs," especially MDMA.

Grouping MDMA with GHB and Rohypnol, a 2000 Knight Ridder story warned that the dangers of "club drugs" include "vulnerability to sexual assault." Similarly, the *Chicago Tribune* cited Ecstasy as the most popular "club drug" before referring to "women who suspect they were raped after they used or were slipped a club drug." In a *Columbus Dispatch* op-ed piece, pediatrician Peter D. Rogers further obscured the distinction between MDMA and the so-called rape drugs by saying that "Ectasy . . . comes in three forms," including "GHB, also called liquid Ecstasy," and "Herbal Ecstasy, also known as ma huang or ephedra" (a legal stimulant), as well as "MDMA, or chemical Ecstasy." He asserted, without citing a source, that "so-called Ecstasy"—it's not clear which one he meant—"has been implicated nationally in the sexual assaults of approximately 5,000 teen-age and young adult women." Rogers described a 16-year-old patient who "took Ecstasy and was raped twice. She told me that she remembers the rapes but, high on the drug, was powerless to stop them. She couldn't even scream, let alone fight back." If Rogers, identified as a member of the American Academy of Pediatrics' Committee on Substance Abuse, had trouble keeping the "club drugs" straight, it's not surprising that the general public saw little difference between giving a date MDMA and slipping her a mickey.

The desire is emotional

As the alleged connections between MDMA and sex illustrate, the concept of an aphrodisiac is complex and ambiguous. A drug could be considered an aphrodisiac because it reduces resistance, because it increases interest, because it improves ability, or because it enhances enjoyment. A particular drug could be effective for one or two of these purposes but useless (or worse) for the others. Shakespeare observed that alcohol "provokes the desire, but it takes away the performance."

Something similar seems to be true of MDMA, except that the desire is more emotional than sexual, a sense of closeness that may find expression in sex that is apt to be aborted because of difficulty in getting an erection or reaching orgasm. Also like alcohol, MDMA is blamed for causing people to act against their considered judgment. The concern is not just that people might have casual sex but that they might regret it afterward.

Surely this concern is not entirely misplaced. As the old saw has it, "Candy is dandy, but liquor is quicker." When drinking precedes sex, there may be a fine line between seducing someone and taking advantage, between lowering inhibitions and impairing judgment. But the possibility of crossing that line does not mean that alcohol is nothing but a trick employed by cads. Nor does the possibility of using alcohol to render someone incapable of resistance condemn it as a tool of rapists.

> *The consensus among users seems to be that MDMA's effects are more sensual than sexual.*

The closest thing we have to a genuine aphrodisiac—increasing interest, ability, and enjoyment—is Viagra, the avowed purpose of which is to enable people to have more and better sex. Instead of being deplored as an aid to hedonism, it is widely praised for increasing the net sum of human happiness. Instead of being sold on the sly in dark nightclubs, it's pitched on television by a former Senate majority leader. The difference seems to be that Viagra is viewed as a legitimate medicine, approved by the government and prescribed by doctors.

But as Joann Ellison Rodgers, author of *Drugs and Sexual Behavior*, observes, "there is great unease with the idea of encouraging sexual prowess. . . . At the very least, drugs in the service of sex do seem to subvert or at least trivialize important aspects of sexual experiences, such as love, romance, commitment, trust and health." If we've managed to accept Viagra and (to a lesser extent) alcohol as aphrodisiacs, it may be only because we've projected their darker possibilities onto other substances, of which the "club drugs" are just the latest examples.

Fears of miscegenation

The current worries about raves in some ways resemble the fears once symbolized by the opium den. The country's first anti-opium laws, passed by Western states in the late 19th century, were motivated largely by hostility toward the low-cost Chinese laborers who competed for work with native whites. Supporters of such legislation, together with a sensationalist press, popularized the image of the sinister Chinaman who lured white women into his opium den, turning them into concubines, prostitutes, or sex slaves. Although users generally find that opiates dampen their sex drive, "it was commonly reported that opium smoking aroused sexual desire," writes historian David Court-Wright, "and that some shameless smokers persuaded 'innocent girls to smoke in order to excite their passions and effect their ruin.'" San Francisco authorities lamented that the police "have found white women and Chinamen side by side under the effects of this drug—a humiliating sight to anyone who has anything left of manhood." In 1910 Hamilton Wright, a U.S. diplomat who was a key player in the passage of federal anti-drug legislation, told Congress that "one of the most unfortunate phases of the habit of smoking opium in this country" was "the large number of women who [had] become involved and were living as common-law wives or cohabiting with Chinese in the Chinatowns of our various cities."

Fears of miscegenation also played a role in popular outrage about cocaine, which was said to make blacks uppity and prone to violence against whites, especially sexual assault. In 1910 Christopher Koch, a member of the Pennsylvania Pharmacy Board who pushed for a federal ban on cocaine, informed Congress that "the colored people seem to have a weakness for it. . . . They would just as leave rape a woman as anything else, and a great many of the southern rape cases have been traced to cocaine." Describing cocaine's effect on "hitherto inoffensive, law abiding negroes" in the *Medical Record*, Edward Huntington Williams warned that "sexual desires are increased and perverted."

> **"** *For most people, MDMA turns off the ability to function as a lover.* **"**

Marijuana, another drug that was believed to cause violence, was also linked to sex crimes and, like opium, seduction. Under marijuana's influence, according to a widely cited 1932 report in *The Journal of Criminal Law and Criminology*, "sexual desires are stimulated and may lead to unnatural acts, such as indecent exposure and rape." The authors quoted an informant who "reported several instances of which he claimed to have positive knowledge, where boys had induced girls to use the weed for the purpose of seducing them." The federal Bureau of Narcotics, which collected anecdotes about marijuana's baneful effects to support a national ban on the drug, cited "colored students at the Univ. of Minn. partying with female students (white) smoking [marijuana] and getting their sympathy with stories of racial persecution. Result pregnancy." The bureau also described a case in which "two Negroes took a girl fourteen years old and kept her for two days in a hut under the influence of marijuana. Upon recovery she was found to be suffering from syphilis."

Drug-related horror stories nowadays are rarely so explicitly racist. A notable and surprising exception appears in the 2000 film *Traffic*, which is critical of the war on drugs but nevertheless represents the utter degradation of an upper-middle-class white teenager who gets hooked on crack by showing her having sex with a black man. Whether related to race or not, parental anxieties about sexual activity among teenagers have not gone away, and drugs are a convenient scapegoat when kids seem to be growing up too fast.

Drugs, sex, and the '60s

The link between drugs and sex was reinforced by the free-love ethos of the '60s counterculture that embraced marijuana and LSD. In the public mind, pot smoking, acid dropping, and promiscuous sex were all part of the same lifestyle; a chaste hippie chick was a contradiction in terms. When Timothy Leary extolled LSD's sex-enhancing qualities in a 1966 interview with *Playboy*, he fueled the fears of parents who worried that their daughters would be seduced into a decadent world of sex, drugs, and rock 'n' roll. The Charles Manson case added a sinister twist to this scenario, raising the possibility of losing one's daughter to an evil cult leader who uses LSD to brainwash his followers, in much the same way as Chinese men were once imagined to enthrall formerly respectable white girls with opium.

The alarm about the sexual repercussions of "club drugs," then, has to be understood in the context of warnings about other alleged aphrodisiacs, often identified with particular groups perceived as inferior, threatening, or both. The fear of uncontrolled sexual impulses, of the chaos that would result if we let our basic instincts run wild, is projected onto these groups and, by extension, their intoxicants. In the case of "club drugs," adolescents are both victims and perpetrators. Parents fear for their children, but they also fear them. When Mayor

Daley warned that "they are after all of our children," he may have been imagining predators in the mold of Fu Manchu or Charles Manson. But the reality is that raves—which grew out of the British "acid house" movement, itself reminiscent of the psychedelic dance scene that emerged in San Francisco during the late '60s—are overwhelmingly a youth phenomenon.

> *[MDMA] is a love drug but not a sex drug for most people.*

The experience of moving all night to a throbbing beat amid flickering light has been likened to tribal dancing around a fire. But for most people over 30, the appeal of dancing for hours on end to the fast, repetitive rhythm of techno music is hard to fathom. "The sensationalist reaction that greets every mention of the word Ecstasy in this country is part of a wider, almost unconscious fear of young people," writes Jonathan Keane in the British *New Statesman*, and the observation applies equally to the United States. For "middle-aged and middle-class opinion leaders . . . E is a symbol of a youth culture they don't understand."

This is not to say that no one ever felt horny after taking MDMA. Individual reactions to drugs are highly variable, and one could probably find anecdotes suggesting aphrodisiac properties for almost any psychoactive substance. And it is no doubt true that some MDMA users, like the woman quoted in *Cosmo*, have paired up with sexual partners they found less attractive the morning after. But once MDMA is stripped of its symbolism, these issues are no different from those raised by alcohol. In fact, since MDMA users tend to be more lucid than drinkers, the chances that they will do something regrettable are probably lower.

Inappropriate emotional intimacy

Another alcohol-related hazard, one that seems to be more characteristic of MDMA than the risk of casual sex or rape, is the possibility of inappropriate emotional intimacy. The maudlin drunk who proclaims his affection for everyone and reveals secrets he might later wish he had kept is a widely recognized character, either comical or pathetic depending upon one's point of view. Given MDMA's reputation as a "love drug," it's natural to wonder whether it fosters the same sort of embarrassing behavior. . . .

"I was very alert but very relaxed at the same time," says Alison Witt, a software engineer in her 20s [All names of drug users have been changed]. "I didn't love everybody. . . . It's a very social drug, and you do feel connected to other people, but I think it's more because it creates a sense of relaxation and pleasure with people you're familiar with." Walter Stevenson, a neuroscientist in his late 20s, gives a similar account: "I felt really happy to have my friends around me. I just enjoyed sitting there and spending time with them, not necessarily talking about anything, but not to the degree that I felt particularly attracted or warm to people I didn't know. I was very friendly and open to meeting people, but there wasn't anything inappropriate about the feeling. . . ."

Not surprisingly, people who use MDMA in clubs and at raves emphasize its sensual and stimulant properties, the way it enhances music and dancing. But they also talk about a sense of connectedness, especially at raves. Jasmine Menendez, a public relations director in her early 20s who has used MDMA both at raves and with small groups of friends, says it provides "a great body high. I lose all sense of inhibition and my full potential is released. . . . It allows me to get closer to people and to myself."

Euphoria is a commonly reported effect of MDMA, which raises the usual concerns about the lure of artificial pleasure. "It was an incredible feeling of being tremendously happy where I was and being content in a basic way," Stevenson recalls of the first time he felt MDMA's effects. He used it several more times after that, but it never became a regular habit. . . .

Sustained use is rare

Sustained heavy use of MDMA is rare, partly because it's impractical. MDMA works mainly by stimulating the release of the neurotransmitter serotonin. Taking it depletes the brain's supply, which may not return to normal levels for a week or more. Some users report a hangover period of melancholy and woolly-headedness that can last a few days. As frequency of use increases, MDMA's euphoric and empathetic effects diminish and its unpleasant side effects, including jitteriness and hangovers, intensify. Like LSD, it has a self-limiting quality, which is reflected in patterns of use. In a 2000 survey, 8.2 percent of high school seniors reported trying MDMA in the previous year. Less than half of them (3.6 percent) had used it in the previous month, and virtually none reported "daily" use (defined as use on 20 or more occasions in the previous 30 days). To parents, of course, any use of MDMA is alarming, and the share of seniors who said they'd ever tried the drug nearly doubled between 1996 and 2000. . . .

> *The alarm about . . . 'club drugs,' . . . has to be understood in the context of warnings about other alleged aphrodisiacs, often identified with . . . groups perceived as . . . threatening.*

Parental fears have been stoked by reports of sudden fatalities among MDMA users. Given the millions of doses consumed each year, such cases are remarkably rare: The Drug Abuse Warning Network counted nine MDMA-related deaths in 1998. The most common cause of death is dehydration and overheating. MDMA impairs body temperature regulation and accelerates fluid loss, which can be especially dangerous for people dancing vigorously in crowded, poorly ventilated spaces for hours at a time. The solution to this problem, well known to experienced ravers, is pretty straightforward: avoid clubs and parties where conditions are stifling, take frequent rests, abstain from alcohol (which compounds dehydration), and drink plenty of water. MDMA also interacts dangerously with some prescription drugs (including monoamine oxidase inhibitors, a class of antidepressants), and it raises heart rate and blood pressure, of special concern for people with cardiovascular conditions.

Another hazard is a product of the black market created by prohibition: Tablets or capsules sold as Ecstasy may in fact contain other, possibly more dangerous drugs. In tests by private U.S. laboratories, more than one-third of "Ecstasy" pills turned out to be bogus. (The samples were not necessarily representative, and the results may be on the high side, since the drugs were submitted voluntarily for testing, perhaps by buyers who had reason to be suspicious.) Most of the MDMA substitutes, which included caffeine, ephedrine, and aspirin, were relatively harmless, but one of them, the cough suppressant dextromethorphan (DXM), has disturbing psychoactive effects in high doses, impedes the metabolism of MDMA, and blocks perspiration, raising the risk of overheating. Another drug that has been passed off as MDMA is paramethoxyamphetamine (PMA), which is potentially lethal in doses over 50 milligrams, especially when combined with other drugs. In 2000 the DEA reported 10 deaths tied to PMA. Wary Ecstasy users can buy test kits or have pills analyzed by organizations such as DanceSafe, which sets up booths at raves and nightclubs.

The dangers of long-term damage

Generally speaking, a careful user can avoid the short-term dangers of MDMA. Of more concern is the possibility of long-term brain damage. In animal studies, high or repeated doses of MDMA cause degeneration of serotonin nerve receptors, and some of the changes appear to be permanent. The relevance of these studies to human use of MDMA is unclear because we don't know whether the same changes occur in people or, if they do, at what doses and with what practical consequences. Studies of human users, which often have serious methodological shortcomings, so far have been inconclusive.

> *Since MDMA users tend to be more lucid than drinkers, the chances that they will do something regrettable are probably lower.*

Still, the possibility of lasting damage to memory should not be lightly dismissed. There's enough reason for concern that MDMA should no longer be treated as casually as "a low-calorie martini." If the fears of neurotoxicity prove to be well founded and a safe dose cannot be estimated with any confidence, a prudent person would need a good reason—probably better than a fun night out—to take the risk. On the other hand, the animal research suggests that it may be possible to avoid neural damage by preventing hyperthermia or by taking certain drugs (for example, Prozac) in conjunction with MDMA. In that case, such precautions would be a requirement of responsible use.

However the debate about MDMA'S long-term effects turns

out, we should be wary of claims that it (or any drug) makes people "engage in random sex acts." Like the idea that certain intoxicants make people lazy, crazy, or violent, it vastly oversimplifies a complex interaction between the drug, the user, and the context. As MDMA's versatility demonstrates, the same drug can be different things to different people. Michael Buchanan, a retired professor in his early 70s, has used MDMA several times with one or two other people. "It's just wonderful," he says, "to bring closeness, intimacy—not erotic intimacy at all, but a kind of spiritual intimacy, a loving relationship, an openness to dialogue that nothing else can quite match." When I mention MDMA use at raves, he says, "I don't understand how the kids can use it that way."

8

Ecstasy May Help Parkinson's Disease Sufferers

Jonathan Margolis

Jonathan Margolis is a British journalist and the author of A Brief History of Tomorrow.

British actor Tim Lawrence tried Ecstasy at a dance club and accidentally discovered that it helped control his Parkinson's symptoms. British researchers are investigating therapeutic use of the drug, perhaps in combination with L-dopa, the medication currently used for Parkinson's treatment.

British film stuntman Tim Lawrence was only 34 when he was diagnosed with the debilitating neurological condition Parkinson's disease six years ago. It meant a swift end not just to his parts in movies like *Braveheart, Splitting Heirs* and *Frankenstein*, but also to an active lifestyle that included acrobatics, martial arts and skydiving. With his body alternating between rigidity and uncontrollable spasms, almost the only physical recreation left for Lawrence was going out with friends to London clubs. Under the strobe lights his thrashing movements could be mistaken for enthusiastic dancing. So clubs became the one place he didn't feel self-conscious.

It was at such a club three years ago that Lawrence took the illegal drug ecstasy. What happened next is promising to turn established theories about Parkinson's disease on their head.

While experts still warn strongly against Parkinson's sufferers taking ecstasy, Lawrence may have stumbled accidentally on the nearest thing yet to a reliable treatment for the disease, which afflicts an estimated 4 million people worldwide. Within half an hour of taking ecstasy, Lawrence felt more than just the sense of elation users of the drug experience. For the first time in years, he regained control of his body, and he retained it until the next morning. "It was like a Road to Damascus," he told *TIME*. "I was suddenly looking down at my body aware that the twitching had gone, and I had this incredible fluidity. I was completely normal."

At first, Lawrence regarded the episode as a freak occurrence. The symptoms of Parkinson's are notoriously unpredictable, and it seemed like just another of the disease's erratic turns. But then he tried ecstasy again, and once more he was able for hours at a time to regain something close to the athletic grace he once possessed. Yet when he mentioned the experience to his doctors, they dismissed it as a result of the street drug's known amphetamine qualities. So Lawrence thought little more about it, other than to make the most of ecstasy's unexpected side effect the couple of times a month he went clubbing. He also kept quiet about his chance discovery, since, in Britain as in many countries, taking the drug is a criminal offense as serious as using heroin or crack cocaine.

> *Within half an hour of taking ecstasy, [Tim] Lawrence . . . regained control of his body, and he retained it until the next morning.*

Now, however, Lawrence's discovery is being hailed as the beginning of a medical breakthrough. After seeing footage from a forthcoming BBC television documentary, two leading Parkinson's researchers have begun full-time investigation into why ecstasy has such a dramatic effect on his condition. The documentary, to be aired this week [February 19, 2001], shows Lawrence in a gym doing forward rolls, somersaults, backflips and swallow dives despite his debilitating condition. The researchers, Professor Alan R. Crossman and Dr. Jonathan M. Brotchie of the University of Manchester, are trying to find a component of the banned substance that might be developed into a safe drug to mimic ecstasy's good effects while suppressing the bad, which include memory loss, brain cell death and depression. And they think such a safe drug could be available for testing within a year.[1]

Parkinson's is an incurable disorder of the central nervous system usually associated with the elderly but now increasingly affecting younger people. Sufferers include Muhammad Ali, Billy Graham, Janet Reno and, according to some reports, the Pope. But research into Parkinson's remained underfunded and under-publicized until actor Michael J. Fox announced he had the disease in 1998, having developed it a decade ago at age 30.

> **"** *Leading Parkinson's researchers have begun full-time investigation into why ecstasy has such a dramatic effect on [this] condition.* **"**

Parkinson's is caused by a breakdown of the brain's production of the neurotransmitter dopamine, which relays the electrical impulses involved in muscular movement. The last great breakthrough in treatment was in the late 1960s, when the "miracle" drug levadopa, or L-dopa—the chemical precursor of dopamine—was discovered to "unfreeze" patients who for decades had been practically rigid, unable even to produce facial expressions. Though it remains the standard treatment for Parkinson's, there is a serious downside to L-dopa. After a couple of years, during which patients seem to be cured, they start developing the jerky, uncontrolled twitching and tremors that most people today associate with Parkinson's.

In a healthy person, natural dopamine is released in tune with the body's needs, but using L-dopa is the equivalent of running a car's turbocharger in traffic. The result for Parkinson's patients is that their condition oscillates between hyperactivity while they are on L-dopa and immobility when they are not. Pharmacologists have been searching for 30 years for a drug to combine effectively with L-dopa and mute the turbocharger effect, but none has emerged.

Ecstasy is an amphetamine-like drug that affects emotions by boosting levels of another neurotransmitter, serotonin,

---

1. As this volume went to press, this drug had not yet been made available.

which is normally connected with feeling happy. Serotonin has rarely been associated with muscular movement. Confusingly for the researchers, scans of Lawrence's brain show that ecstasy has a beneficial effect on his Parkinson's even when he takes it on its own, without L-dopa.

Researchers around the world, including Crossman and Brotchie, have suspected that serotonin may have some connection with Parkinson's and have been searching for a serotonin-stimulating drug to combine with L-dopa. They have had little success, though, and the news that the missing link may be ecstasy, or at least something in it, has cheered the Manchester duo. "The reason we're excited by Tim's case is that we've spent between us the best part of 50 years trying to understand movement disorders, and the effect we see in him with MDMA [ecstasy's scientific name] is the biggest we've ever seen," says Brotchie. "Ecstasy on its own isn't going to be a useful treatment. But the potential may now be there to develop completely new drugs for Parkinson's."

Brotchie's enthusiasm is shared by Dr. Thomas N. Chase, a neurologist who heads the experimental therapeutics branch of the National Institutes of Health in Bethesda, Maryland. "We don't work with street drugs, but we are not averse to taking clues from all sources," Chase says. "Parkinson's is a condition for which there is no adequate therapy, so if this observation with ecstasy is reliable, it could lead to a line of research which could benefit many, many people with this disease. And my guess is that this observation will pay off."

It was by chance that Lawrence's case came to the notice of researchers at all. Documentary director Jemima Harrison of Carlton Television, which produced the BBC documentary, was making what looked like a routine report on Parkinson's research, A friend of hers had recommended Lawrence as an especially articulate sufferer. "We were talking about filming him trying a new surgical technique in Spain," says Harrison. "Then one day I asked him out of curiosity if cannabis helped him at all. He said no, and I nosily asked if he'd tried any other drugs. He said, 'Well, I occasionally take ecstasy, and it renders me completely normal for several hours.' So I started looking up the science, and it seemed impossible for ecstasy to have that effect. That's where it started getting interesting."

Lawrence is uneasy about his impending celebrity: the former British soldier's views on drug use are far from libertarian. "Other people take ecstasy because they want to be in an impassive state, have a different perception listening to music and to dance all night. I do it to experience normality. But I also feel the heightened sensory perception, and I wouldn't want to be experiencing that on a daily basis because you wouldn't get anything else done. So if there is an outcry over my using ecstasy, if I was investigated and if people were really anti, I'd have to be a bit more careful." Yet if the research Lawrence has inspired somehow does pay off, nobody is likely to fault him simply for wanting to dance.

9

Anti–Club Drug Laws Help Stop Drug Abuse

Bob Graham

Bob Graham is a U.S. senator. He was formerly the governor of Florida.

The Ecstasy Prevention Act of 2001 provides federal and local authorities help in combating the trafficking, distribution, and abuse of Ecstasy and other club drugs. It provides funding for educational programs that explain the serious risks associated with club drug use. The act also allows communities that have passed ordinances against Ecstasy and other club drugs to obtain federal grants.

Editor's Note: The following viewpoint was originally presented to the U.S. Senate on July 19, 2001, in support of the Ecstasy Prevention Act of 2001. The act did not pass, but it was replaced by the Illicit Drug Anti-Proliferation Act, which passed in 2003.

I rise today, along with my colleagues, Senators [Charles E.] GRASSLEY, [Joseph] LIEBERMAN, [Dick] DURBIN, [Mary] LANDRIEU, and [Hillary] CLINTON, to introduce the Ecstasy Prevention Act of 2001; legislation to combat the recent rise in trafficking, distribution and violence associated with MDMA, a club drug commonly known as Ecstasy. Ecstasy has become the "feel good" drug of choice among many of our young people, and drug pushers are marketing it as a "friendly" drug to mostly teenagers and young adults.

Last year [2000] I sponsored and Congress passed legislation

Bob Graham, statement before the Senate Committee on the Judiciary, Washington, DC, July 19, 2001.

which drew attention to the dangers of Ecstasy and strengthened the penalties attached to trafficking in Ecstasy and other "club drugs." Since then, Ecstasy use and trafficking continue to grow at epidemic proportions, and there are many accounts of deaths and permanent damage to the health of those who use Ecstasy. The U.S. Customs Service continues to report large increases in Ecstasy seizures, over 9 million pills were seized by Customs last year, a dramatic rise from the 400,000 seized in 1997. According to the United States Customs Service in Fiscal Year 2001, two individual seizures affected by Customs Inspectors in Miami, FL totaled approximately 422,000 ecstasy tablets. These two seizures alone exceeded the entire amount of ecstasy seized by the Customs Service in all of Fiscal Year 1997. The Deputy Director of Office of National Drug Control Policy, ONDCP, Dr. Donald Vereen, Jr., M.D., M.P.H., recently said that "Ecstasy is one of the most problematic drugs that has emerged in recent years." The National Drug Intelligence Center, in its most recent publication *Threat Assessment 2001*, has noted that "no drug in the Other Dangerous Drugs Category represents a more immediate threat than MDMA" or Ecstasy.

Ecstasy use is increasing

The Office of National Drug Control Policy's *Year 2000 Annual Report on the National Drug Control Strategy* clearly states that the use of Ecstasy is on the rise in the United States, particularly among teenagers and young professionals. My State of Florida has been particularly hard hit by this plague, but so have the States of many of my colleagues here. Ecstasy is customarily sold and consumed at "raves," which are semi-clandestine, all-night parties and concerts. Numerous data also reflect the increasing availability of ecstasy in metropolitan centers and suburban communities. In the most recent release of *Pulse Check: Trends in Drug Abuse Mid-year 2000*, which featured MDMA and club drugs, it was reported that the sale and use of club drugs have expanded from raves and nightclubs to high schools, streets, neighborhoods and other open venues.

Not only has the use of Ecstasy exploded, more than doubling among 12th graders in the last two years, but it has also spread well beyond its origin as a party drug for affluent white suburban teenagers to virtually every ethnic and class group, and from big cities like New York and Los Angeles to rural Vermont and South Dakota.

And now, this year, law enforcement officials say they are seeing another worrisome development, increasingly violent turf wars among Ecstasy dealers, and some of those dealers are our young people. Homicides linked to Ecstasy dealing have occurred in recent months in Norfolk, VA, Elgin, IL, near Chicago; and in Valley Stream, NY. Police suspect Ecstasy in other murders in the suburbs, of Washington, DC, and Los Angeles, and violence is being linked to Israeli drug dealers in Los Angeles and to organized crime in New York City. Ecstasy is also becoming widely available on the Internet. Last year, a man arrested in Orlando, FL, had been selling Ecstasy to customers in New York.

> *Ecstasy is an extremely dangerous drug.*

The lucrative nature of Ecstasy encourages its importation. Production costs are as low as two to twenty-five cents per dose while retail prices in the U.S. range from twenty dollars to $45 per dose. Manufactured mostly in Europe, in nations such as the Netherlands, Belgium, and Spain where pill presses are not controlled as they are in the U.S., ecstasy has erased all of the old routes law enforcement has mapped out for the smuggling of traditional drugs. And now the trade is being promoted by organized criminal elements, both from abroad and here. Although Israeli and Russian groups dominate MDMA smuggling, the involvement of domestic groups appears to be increasing. Criminal groups based in Chicago, Phoenix, Texas, and Florida have reportedly secured their own sources of supply in Europe.

Ecstasy is dangerous

Young Americans are being lulled into a belief that ecstasy, and other designer drugs are "safe" ways to get high, escape reality, and enhance intimacy in personal relationships. The drug traffickers make their living off of perpetuating and exploiting this myth.

I want to be perfectly clear in stating that ecstasy is an extremely dangerous drug. In my State alone, between July and December of last year, there were 25 deaths in which MDMA or a variant were listed as a cause of death, and there were another

25 deaths where MDMA was present in the toxicology, although not actually listed as the cause of death. This drug is a definite killer.

The "Ecstasy Prevention Act of 2001" renews and enhances our commitment toward fighting the proliferation and trafficking of Ecstasy and other club drugs. It builds on last year's Ecstasy Anti-Proliferation Act of 2000 and provides legislation to assist the Federal and local organizations that are fighting to stop this potentially life-threatening drug. This legislation will allot funding for programs that will educate law enforcement officials and young people and will assist community-based anti-drug efforts. To that end, this bill amends Section 506B(c) of title V of the Public Health Service Act, by adding that priority of funding should be given to communities that have taken measures to combat club drug trafficking and use, to include passing ordinances and increasing law enforcement on Ecstasy.

The bill also provides money for the National Institute on Drug Abuse to conduct research and evaluate the effects that MDMA or Ecstasy has on an individual's health. And, because there is a fear that the lack of current drug tests ability to screen for Ecstasy may encourage Ecstasy use over other drugs, the bill directs ONDCP to commission a test for Ecstasy that meets the standards of and can be used in the Federal Workplace.

Through this campaign, our hope is that Ecstasy will soon go the way of crack, which saw a dramatic reduction in the quantities present on our streets after information of its unpredictable impurities and side effects were made known to a wide audience. By using this educational effort we hope to avoid future deaths and ruined lives.

The Ecstasy Prevention Act of 2000 can only help in our fight against drug abuse in the United States. Customs is working hard to stem the flow of Ecstasy into our country. As legislators we have a responsibility to stop the proliferation of this potentially life threatening drug. The Ecstasy Prevention Act of 2001 will assist the Federal and local agencies charged to fight drug abuse by raising the public profile on the substance-abuse challenge posed by the increasing availability and use of Ecstasy and by focusing on the serious danger it presents to our youth.

We urge our colleagues in the Senate to join us in this important effort by co-sponsoring this bill.

10

Anti–Club Drug Laws Will Prove to Be Ineffective

Center for Cognitive Liberty and Ethics

The Center for Cognitive Liberty and Ethics (CCLE) is a research and policy center that seeks to develop and enhance social policies that preserve and encourage freedom of thought in the twenty-first century. The CCLE believes that the most beneficial application and regulation of new drugs and neurotechnologies will be discovered through allegiance to the fundamental right to freedom of thought.

The Ecstasy Prevention Act of 2001 will prove to be ineffective and will violate civil liberties. It encourages scare rhetoric exaggerating the dangers associated with club drug use rather than providing accurate information about the harms and benefits of such use. Further, the act provides funding for law enforcement to incarcerate users and dealers of club drugs, which will result in the jailing of an increasing number of otherwise law-abiding citizens who use those drugs without causing harm to others. People have the right to use club drugs so long as their behavior does not present a danger to others.

Editor's Note: The Ecstasy Prevention Act of 2001 did not pass. However, it was replaced by the Illicit Drug Anti-Proliferation Act, which passed in 2003.

On July 19, 2001, in conjunction with a 2-day [National Institute on Drug Abuse] directed Ecstasy conference, Senator Bob Graham (D-Fla) introduced the "Ecstasy Prevention Act of 2001" (S. 1208). An almost identical bill (H.R. 2582), with the same title, was introduced the following day in the House of Representatives by Representative John Mica (R-Fla).

On December 20, 2001, the Ecstasy Prevention Act of 2001 was attached by amendment to the 21st Century Department of Justice Appropriations Authorization Act (H.R. 2215), and passed the Senate. The Ecstasy Prevention Act is found within H.R. 2215, at Title VIII (Secs. 8001-8007).

This is a brief summary and analysis of the major provisions of the Ecstasy Prevention Act of 2001, as attached to H.R. 2215.

Major provisions of the act

Under Section 8002 of the Act, communities that pass ordinances "restricting rave clubs" and increase law enforcement efforts directed toward Ecstasy offenses, will receive priority in obtaining federal grants under the Public Health Service Act.

Analysis: Targeting "rave clubs" in an effort to crack down on MDMA use is analogous to targeting anyone with long hair or a tie-died shirt for marijuana possession. Use of such profiling unconstitutionally elevates cultural stereotypes to the level of probable cause. The fact that federal anti-drug agents have to rely on music profiling to enforce anti-MDMA drug laws reveals that the vast majority of people who use MDMA do so responsibly and cannot be identified based on violent or anti-social behavior. Instead, in order to crack down on MDMA use, the police are reduced to employing overbroad profiles based on the style of music certain people listen to.

The U.S. government should not be allocating public health funds based on a community's capitulation to federal government pressures coercing them to squelch a particular entertainment subculture. Advancing public health is better accomplished by providing people with truthful information about illegal drugs, and allocating money for harm reduction programs.

Sections 8003 and 8007 of the Act authorize the use of government funds ($15 million in the original bill) "to assist anti-Ecstasy law enforcement initiatives in high intensity drug trafficking areas" and (another $1 million in the original bill) to establish a federal "Task Force on Ecstasy/MDMA and Emerging

Club Drugs," which will report to President [George W.] Bush and to Congress on how to improve national drug control strategy with regard to Ecstasy.

Analysis: According to the United Nations, 180 million people—worldwide—use illegal drugs. The National Drug Intelligence Center reports that 3.3 million Americans admitted in 1998 that they have used MDMA at some point in their lives, and last year [2000] U.S. Customs seized 9.3 million MDMA pills. Currently, over 2 million Americans are incarcerated in the U.S. with 299,000 serving time for drug offenses.

Such statistics show that the desire to experience alternative states of consciousness is widespread, and will never be policed out of existence no matter how much money is allocated to the cause. Rather than spend an additional $16 million on the futile and immoral task of policing peoples' *mental states,* the U.S. government should consider employing a harm-based national drug policy; one that polices people whose *behavior,* after taking a drug such as MDMA, actually causes harm to others or presents a clear and present danger to others.

> *The desire to experience alternative states of consciousness is widespread, and will never be policed out of existence.*

Not only would such a harm-based policy save hundreds of millions of dollars, it would return a morally defensible foundation to national drug policy. What goes on inside one's head is just as private as what goes on inside one's bedroom. A person who responsibly alters his or her consciousness (with the use of MDMA or any other drug, technique, or technology) should be left in peace unless his or her subsequent behavior endangers others.

A scare campaign

Under Section 8004 of the Act, the Director of ONDCP [Office of National Drug Control Policy] is ordered to ensure that the "national youth anti-drug media campaign" that "addresses the reduction and prevention of abuse of MDMA and emerging drugs among young people in the United States."

Analysis: This section of the Act seeks to bolster an unabashed scare campaign under the guise of drug education. Americans and their children are not served by bombarding them with additional Drug War propaganda. Presenting further scare-rhetoric, rather than providing accurate information about the potential harms and benefits of a drug like MDMA, is not only ineffective, it is dangerously irresponsible. Americans and their children should be told the truth about drugs by their government, including providing potentially life-saving facts about how to minimize the harm that may be associated with taking MDMA.

Under Section 8005 of the Act, the Office of National Drug Control Policy (ONDCP) can authorize "such sums as are necessary . . . to commission a drug test for MDMA which would meet the standards for the Federal Workplace."

Analysis. The testing of American's bodily fluids for illegal drugs is a $1 billion industry. There is no government research suggesting that federal workers are under the influence of MDMA in the workplace. Allocating federal money to produce a drug test for MDMA that can be used to probe the bodily fluids of employees is a disguised effort to detect and police their use of MDMA *in their off-work, private hours.* Federal workers should be judged based on their performance on the job, not based on personal, private, leisure time decisions.

> *Presenting . . . scare-rhetoric, rather than providing accurate information about the potential harms and benefits of a drug like MDMA . . . is dangerously irresponsible.*

The vast majority of adults use drugs responsibly—whether the drug is legal like alcohol, and Vicodin, or illegal like marijuana and MDMA. Indeed, were it not for a host of invasive law enforcement tactics and tools, including drug testing, it would be almost impossible for the government to determine who is using illegal drugs and who is not. Since there is no evidence that MDMA use is occurring in the federal work place, this provision should be recognized as a further allocation of money to increase the policing of Americans' private mental states, under the guise of providing a "drug free" workplace.

Under Section 8006 of the Act, the National Institute on Drug Abuse (NIDA) is ordered to conduct research on MDMA and to publish a public report that "evaluates the effects that MDMA use can have on an individual's health," and documents "those research findings with respect to MDMA that are scientifically valid and identify the medical consequences on an individual's health."

Analysis: As a government agency playing a major role in waging the War on Drugs, the National Institute on Drug Abuse (NIDA) has, unfortunately, become an agent of ideology, rather than a neutral scientific advisor. This is made clear by examining the presenters at the most recent NIDA conference on MDMA, which took place on July 19, 20, 2001. Well-respected researchers such as Dr. David Nichols (Professor of Medicinal Chemistry and Pharmacology from Purdue University) and Dr. Charles Grob (Professor of Psychiatry at the UCLA School of Medicine) were not invited, because their research and clinical findings with respect to MDMA present *balanced* examinations of MDMA—examinations that address both the potential health consequences of MDMA as well as the drug's potential benefits in a therapeutic setting.

More research on MDMA's health consequences and potential benefits is needed, but it should not be agenda-driven. Unfortunately, in the climate of a government-declared "War on Drugs" *all* government information becomes propagandized. Americans are no longer able to trust government statements about illegal drugs such as MDMA.

Perpetuating a failed policy

The provisions of the Ecstasy Prevention Act of 2001 seek to perpetuate a failed and futile War on Drugs policy, by employing more police and filling more prison cells with otherwise law-abiding citizens who use MDMA without causing harm to others. Pouring more money into policing Americans' mental states is ineffective and a wholly inappropriate government activity. Public health is more effectively advanced by producing and disseminating harm reduction information about MDMA than by coercing communities to prohibit or restrict electronic music events. Lastly, Americans and their children deserve truthful, fact-based information about both the potential dangers and the potential benefits associated with MDMA.

Organizations to Contact

The editors have compiled the following list of organizations concerned with the issues debated in this book. The descriptions are derived from materials provided by the organizations. All have publications or information available for interested readers. The list was compiled on the date of publication of the present volume; names, addresses, phone and fix numbers, and e-mail and Internet addresses may change. Be aware that many organizations take several weeks or longer to respond to inquiries, so allow as much time as possible.

American Council for Drug Education (ACDE)
136 E. Sixty-Fourth St., New York, NY 10163
(800) 488-3784 • fax: (212) 758-6784
e-mail: acde@phoenixhouse.org • Web site: www.acde.org

The American Council for Drug Education informs the public about the harmful effects of abusing drugs and alcohol. It was created by Phoenix House, the largest private substance abuse treatment program in the United States. Among its publications are the Drug Awareness Series of brochures that provide information on illegal drugs.

Canadian Centre on Substance Abuse (CCSA)
75 Albert St., Suite 300, Ottawa, ON K1P 5E7 Canada
(613) 235-4048 • fax: (613) 235-8101
e-mail: info@ccsa.ca • Web site: www.ccsa.ca

The CCSA works to minimize the harm associated with the use of alcohol, tobacco, and other drugs by sponsoring public debates on this issue. It disseminates information on the nature, extent, and consequences of substance abuse and supports organizations involved in substance abuse treatment, prevention, and educational programming. The center publishes the newsletter *Action News*.

Canadian Foundation for Drug Policy (CFDP)
70 MacDonald St., Ottawa, ON K2P 1H6 Canada
(613) 236-1027 • fax: (613) 238-2891
e-mail: eoscapel@fox.nstn.ca • Web site: www.cfdp.ca

Founded by several of Canada's leading drug policy specialists, the CFDP examines the objectives and consequences of Canada's drug laws and policies. When necessary, the foundation recommends alternatives that it believes would make Canada's drug policies more effective and humane. The CFDP discusses drug policy issues with the Canadian government, media, and general public. It also disseminates educational materials and maintains a Web site.

Cato Institute
1000 Massachusetts Ave. NW, Washington, DC 20001-5403
(202) 842-0200
Web site: www.cato.org

The institute is a public policy research foundation dedicated to limiting the control of government and to protecting individual liberty. Cato, which strongly favors drug legalization, publishes the *Cato Journal* three times a year and the *Cato Policy Report* bimonthly.

Center for Cognitive Liberty and Ethics (CCLE)
PO Box 73481, Davis, CA 95617-3481
(530) 750-7912 • fax: (530) 570-7912
e-mail: info@cognitiveliberty.org • Web site: www.cognitiveliberty.org

The Center for Cognitive Liberty and Ethics is a nonprofit organization dedicated to protecting and advancing freedom of thought in the area of neurotechnologies. CCLE works to ensure that the application and regulation of new psychotropic drugs and neurotechnologies proceed with as few restrictions as possible and is consistent with the fundamental right to freedom of thought. CCLE publishes *Mind Matter*, a quarterly newsletter; the *Journal of Cognitive Liberty*, a quarterly journal; various flyers and pamphlets; and maintains a Web site.

Center on Addiction and Substance Abuse (CASA)
Columbia University, 152 W. Fifty-Seventh St., New York, NY 10019
(212) 841-5200 • fax: (212) 956-8020
Web site: www.casacolumbia.org

CASA is a private, nonprofit organization that works to educate the public about the hazards of chemical dependency. The organization supports treatment as the best way to reduce chemical dependency. It produces publications describing the harmful effects of alcohol and drug addiction and effective ways to address the problem of substance abuse. It also distributes the monthly newsletter *START* and maintains a Web site.

DanceSafe
c/o HRC, 22 W. Twenty-Seventh St., 5th Fl., New York, NY 10001
e-mail: dsusa@dancesafe.org • Web site: www.dancesafe.org

DanceSafe is a nonprofit harm reduction organization promoting health and safety within the rave and club communities. It provides information on drugs, safe sex, and other health issues and offers pill testing and adulterant screening. DanceSafe maintains a Web site and an on-line bookstore.

Drug Enforcement Administration (DEA)
700 Army Navy Dr., Arlington, VA 22202
(202) 307-1000
Web site: www.dea.gov

The DEA is the federal agency charged with enforcing the nation's drug laws. The agency concentrates on stopping the smuggling and distribution of narcotics in the United States and abroad. It publishes the *Drug Enforcement Magazine* three times a year.

Drug Policy Alliance
70 W. Thirty-sixth St., 16th Fl., New York, NY 10018
(212) 613-8020 • fax: (212) 613-8021
Web site: www. lindesmith.org

The Drug Policy Alliance is working to broaden the public debate on drug policy and to promote alternatives to the war on drugs based on science, compassion, health and human rights. The Alliance promotes harm reduction, an alternative approach to drug policy and treatment that focuses on minimizing the adverse effects of both drug use and drug prohibition. The Alliance's published research briefs, fact sheets, and articles are available on its Web site.

Drug Policy Foundation
4801 Massachusetts Ave. NW, #400, Washington, DC 20016
(202) 537-5005
Web site: www.dpf.gov

The foundation supports legalizing many drugs and increasing the number of treatment programs for addicts. The foundation's publications include the bimonthly *Drug Policy Letter* and the book *The Great Drug War*. It also distributes *Press Clips*, an annual compilation of newspaper articles on drug legalization issues, as well as legislative updates.

Libertarian Party
1528 Pennsylvania Ave. SE, Washington, DC 20003-3116
(202) 543-1988
Web site: www.lp.org

The Libertarian Party is a political party whose goal is to protect individual rights and liberties. It advocates the repeal of all laws prohibiting the production, sale, possession, or use of drugs. The party believes law enforcement should focus on preventing violent crimes against persons and property rather than on prosecuting people who use drugs. It publishes the bimonthly *Libertarian Party News* and periodic *Issues Papers* and distributes a compilation of articles supporting drug legalization.

Multidisciplinary Association for Psychedelic Studies (MAPS)
2105 Robinson Ave., Sarasota, FL 34232
(941) 924-6277 • fax: (941) 924-6265
e-mail: askmaps@maps.org • Web site: www.maps.org

The Multidisciplinary Association for Psychedelic Studies is a research and educational organization that assists scientists to design, fund, obtain approval for, and report on studies into the risks and benefits of MDMA (Ecstasy), psychedelic drugs, and marijuana. MAPS maintains a Web site and an online bookstore.

National Institute on Drug Abuse (NIDA)
U.S. Department of Health and Human Services
5600 Fishers Ln., Rockville, MD 20857
(301) 443-6245
Web site: www.nida.nih.gov

NIDA supports and conducts research on drug abuse—including the yearly Monitoring the Future Survey—in order to improve addiction prevention, treatment, and policy efforts. It publishes the bimonthly *NIDA Notes* newsletter, the periodic *NIDA Capsules* fact sheets, and a catalog of research reports and public education materials such as *Marijuana: Facts for Teens.*

Office of National Drug Control Policy (ONDCP)
Executive Office of the President, Drugs and Crime Clearinghouse
PO Box 6000, Rockville, MD 20849-6000
Web site: www.whitehousedrugpolicy.gov

The Office of National Drug Control Policy is responsible for formulating the government's national drug strategy and the president's antidrug policy as well as coordinating the federal agencies responsible for stopping drug trafficking. Drug policy studies are available upon request.

RAND Corporation
Distribution Services
1700 Main St., PO Box 2138, Santa Monica, CA 90407-2138
(310) 393-0411, ext. 6686
Web site: www.rand.org

The RAND Corporation is a research institution that seeks to improve public policy through research and analysis. RAND's Drug Policy Research Center publishes information on the costs, prevention, and treatment of alcohol and drug abuse as well as on trends in drug-law enforcement. Its extensive list of publications includes the book *Sealing the Borders*, by Peter Reuter.

Reason Foundation
3451 S. Sepulveda Blvd., Suite 400, Los Angeles, CA 90034
(310) 391-2245
Web site: www.reason.org

This public policy organization researches contemporary social and political problems and promotes libertarian philosophy and free-market principles. It publishes the monthly *Reason* magazine, which contains articles and editorials critical of the war on drugs and smoking regulation.

University of Michigan
426 Thompson, Ann Arbor, MI 48104-2321
(313) 747-4416
Web site: www.isr.umich.edu

The institute conducts the annual Monitoring the Future Survey, which gathers data on drug use—including club drug use—and attitudes toward drugs among eighth-, tenth-, and twelfth-grade students. Survey results are published by the National Institute on Drug Abuse.

Bibliography

Books

Anne Alverque — *Ecstasy: The Danger of False Euphoria.* New York: Rosen, 2000.

Christine Brennan — *Ecstasy and Other Designer Drugs.* Philadelphia: Chelsea House, 2000.

Sean Connolly — *Ecstasy.* Chicago: Heinemann Library, 2001.

Antonio Escohotado — *A Brief History of Drugs: From the Stone Age to the Stoned Age.* Rochester, VT: Park Street Press, 1999.

Jimi Fitz — *Rave Culture, An Insider's Overview.* Victoria, BC, Canada: Smallfry Press, 1999.

Julie Holland — *Ecstasy: The Complete Guide: A Comprehensive Look at the Risks and Benefits.* Rochester, VT: Park Street Press, 2001.

Margaret Oldroyd Hyde — *Drugs 101: An Overview for Teens.* Brookfield, CT: Twenty First Century Books, 2003.

Karl Jansen — *Ketamine: Dreams and Realities.* Sarasota, FL: Multidisciplinary Association for Psychedelic Studies, 2001.

Cynthia R. Knowles — *Up All Night: A Closer Look at Club Drugs and Rave Culture.* San Francisco: Red House Press, 2001.

Cynthia Kuhn — *Buzzed: The Straight Facts About the Most Used Drugs from Alcohol to Ecstasy.* New York: W.W. Norton, 2003.

Sarah Lennad-Brown — *Drugs.* Austin, TX: Raintree Steck-Vaughn, 2002.

Tara McCall — *This Is Not a Rave: In the Shadow of a Subculture.* New York: Thunder's Mouth Press, 2002.

Frank Owen — *Clubland: The Fabulous Rise and Murderous Fall of Club Culture.* New York: St. Martin's Press, 2003.

Simon Reynolds — *Generation Ecstasy: Into the World of Techno and Rave Culture.* New York: Routledge Press, 1999.

Nicholas Sanders et al. — *In Search of the Ultimate High: Spiritual Experience Through Psychoactivites.* London: Trafalgar Square/Rider, 2000.

Brock E. Schroeder — *Ecstasy.* Philadelphia: Chelsea House, 2004.

Mireille Silcott — *Rave America: New School Dancescapes.* Toronto: ECW Press, 1999.

Clare Tattersall	*Date Rape Drugs.* New York: Rosen, 2000.
Myra Weatherly	*Ecstasy and Other Designer Drug Dangers.* Berkeley Heights, NJ: Enslow, 2000.
Scott P. Werther	*Ecstasy and Your Heart: The Incredibly Disgusting Story.* New York: Rosen, 2001.

Periodicals

Melissa Abramovitz	"The Knockout Punch of Date Rape Drugs," *Current Health 2*, March 2001.
AIDS Alert	"Methamphetamine Use Is Heightening Risks Among Gay Youth; Club Drugs Dull Safe-Sex Sensibilities," October 2002.
Arir-Alina Allaste and Mikko Lagerspetz	"Recreational Drug Use in Estonia: The Context of Club Culture," *Contemporary Drug Problem*, Spring 2002.
Kevin Campbell	"The Ecstasy Scare: How to Deal with the New Threat," *Ebony*, November 2002.
Richard S. Cohen	"Ecstasy: The Love Drug," *Gay and Lesbian Review*, July 2001.
Drug Detection Report	"Experts Fight Growth of Myth That Club Drugs Are Harmless," August 9, 2001.
Charles S. Grob	"The Politics of Ecstasy: Is U.S. Drug Policy on Ecstasy Scientifically Justified?" *Journal of Addiction and Mental Health*, March/April 2002.
Paul A.T. Kelly	"Does Recreational Ecstasy Use Cause Long-Term Cognitive Problems?" *Western Journal of Medicine*, August 2000.
Kathliann M. Kowalski	"Club Drugs: Nothing to Rave About," *Current Health*, February 2002.
Mary Ann Marshall	"The Scary Truth About Ecstasy," *Cosmopolitan*, August 2000.
Eric Nagourney	"The Fight Against Ecstasy," *New York Times Upfront*, December 10, 2001.
Nicole Rivard	"Club Drugs Go to College," *Matrix*, September 2002.
Brandon Spun	"Move over Prozac, It's Ecstasy's Turn," *Insight on the News*, April 15, 2002.
Benjamin Wallace-Wells	"The Agony of Ecstasy: How a Suburban Party Diversion Is Becoming a Dangerous Street Drug," *Washington Monthly*, May 2003.

Index

93